Colophon

Concept Andrej Pirrwitz

Design Jimmy Sabater

Text Christoph Tannert

Translation English (pp. 7, 70) & French (pp. 9, 71)
Patrick Kremer

Copy Editing Patrick Kremer, Ernest Fischbauch

Photo Credits © Andrej Pirrwitz

Production Management Xavier Huches

Printing and Binding
Longo AG Spa
www.longo.media

Distribution
Edel Germany GmbH
www.edel.com
international-books@edel.com

ISBN 978-3-95476-341-2
Printed in Europe

Published by
DISTANZ Verlag
www.distanz.de

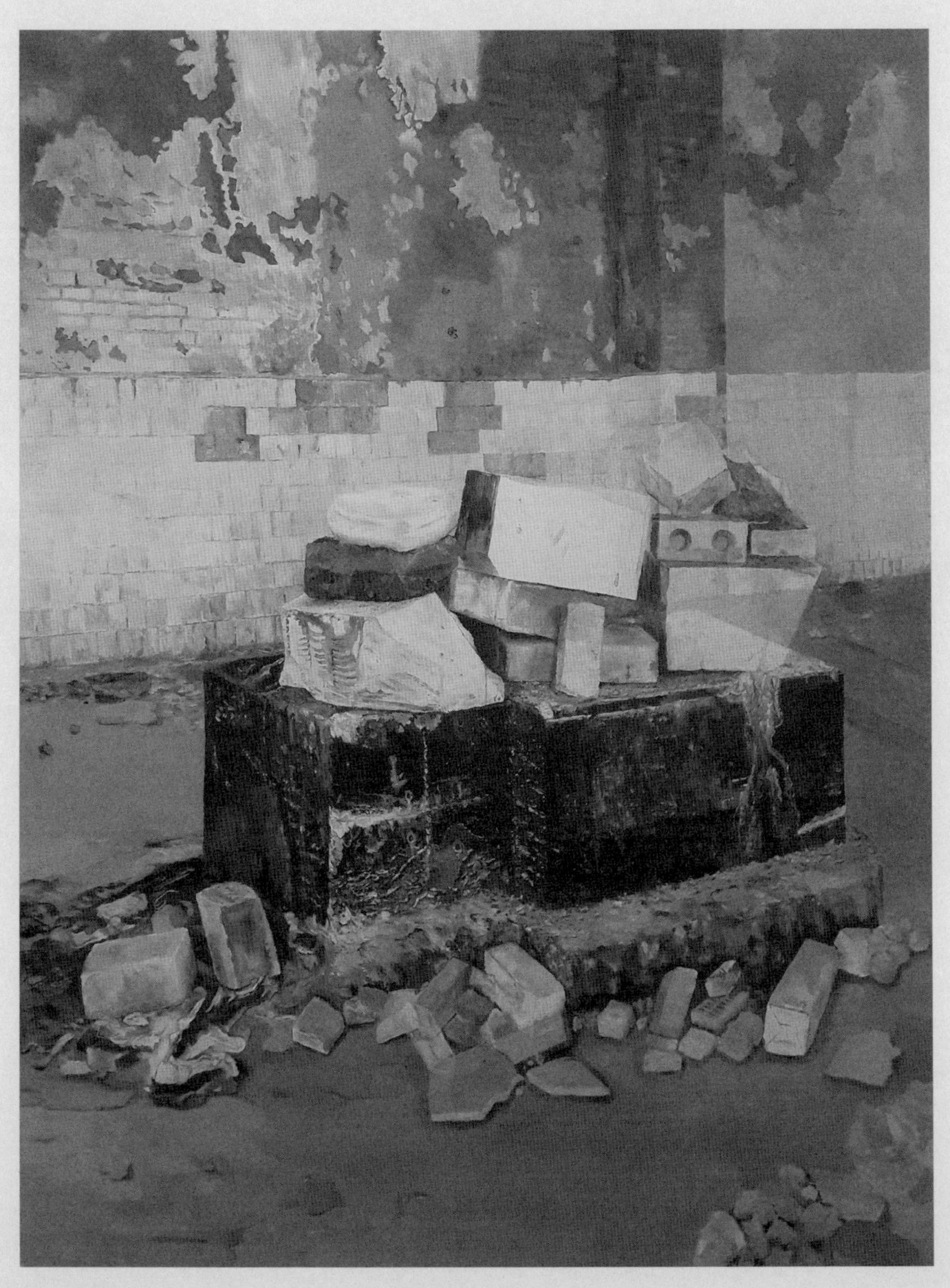

Content

Pietà (monochrome detail, see p. 24) 4-5

Putting Time on Hold, Christoph Tannert 7
Stillstellung der Zeit 8
Suspension du temps 9

Plates – Photographs by Andrej Pirrwitz 13-68

Self-Portrait, 2011, 95 × 123 cm (detail) 13
Falscher Himmel, 2012, 95 × 120 cm 14
Wandelndes Elixier, 2012, 95 × 120 cm 15
apiary, 2012, 95 × 120 cm 16
sky scraper, 2017, 95 × 120 cm 17
Zeigerlosigkeit, 2017, 120 × 150 cm 18-19
schau-Spiel, 2013, 95 × 120 cm 20
Zwielichtiger, 2013, 95 × 120 cm 21
Das Verhör, 2020, 95 × 120 cm 22
my favorite pet, 2015, 95 × 120 cm 23
Pietà, 2019, 120 × 150 cm 24
rhombus, quadrat & kegelstumpf, 2018, 95 × 120 cm 25
§§, 2018, 120 × 150 cm 26
between blue walls, 2018, 95 × 120 cm 27
Kippstuhl, 2020, 120 × 159 cm (detail) 28-29
Thronflüchtiger, 2014, 95 × 120 cm 30
Der Prozeß, 2014, 95 × 120 cm 31
Tischtausch II, 2015, 95 × 120 cm 32
Tischtausch I, 2015, 95 × 120 cm 33
Babel tower III, 2018, 95 × 120 cm 34
Babel tower I, 2018, 95 × 120 cm 35
Zwischen Tür & Angel, 2017, 120 × 150 cm 36
220V, 2018, 95 × 120 cm 37
Des Kaisers neue Kleider, 2019, 95 × 120 cm 38
chess table, 2017, 120 × 130 cm (detail) 39
entropy, 2017, 120 × 150 cm 40
Der seichte Turm, 2018, 95 × 120 cm 41
Monumentbesteigung, 2017, 95 × 120 cm 42
...im falschen Film, 2019, 95 × 120 cm 43
Pb-Schleier, 2015, 95 × 120 cm 44
(Dé)composition, 2018, 95 × 120 cm 45
moloko II, 2012, 120 × 150 cm 46
moloko I, 2012, 120 × 150 cm 47
erstarrte Bresche, 2012, 120 × 150 cm 48
Quadrature en rose, 2019, 120 × 150 cm 49
mostars I, 2015, 97 × 150 cm 50-51
Stille Krönung, 2012, 120 × 150 cm 52
mostars II, 2015, 120 × 150 cm 53
wardrobe pusher II, 2014, 120 × 150 cm 54
good bye Lenin, 2012, 112 × 150 cm 55
Le temoin d´Icarus, 2011, 3 × 80 × 135 cm (triptych) 56-57
Heimlichkeiten, 2019, 120 × 126 cm 58
Schiffe versenken I, 2014, 125 × 125 cm (detail) 59
E-lake, 2016, 120 × 150 cm 60
chateau d' eau, 2016, 120 × 150 cm 61
mise au green, 2016, 95 × 120 cm 62
Kassetten-Korner, 2018, 120 × 150 cm 63
Pizza-Stube, 2013, 95 × 120 cm 64
sitzendes Paar, 2019, 95 × 120 cm 65
nature morte I, 2013, 95 × 120 cm 66
nature morte II, 2017, 95 × 120 cm 67
Schach-matt II, 2020, 95 × 120 cm 68

Biography 70-71

Großer Frieden, 2014, oil on canvas (monochrome detail) 73

Public Collections, Publications 74

Krönung, 2020, oil on canvas (monochrome image) 78

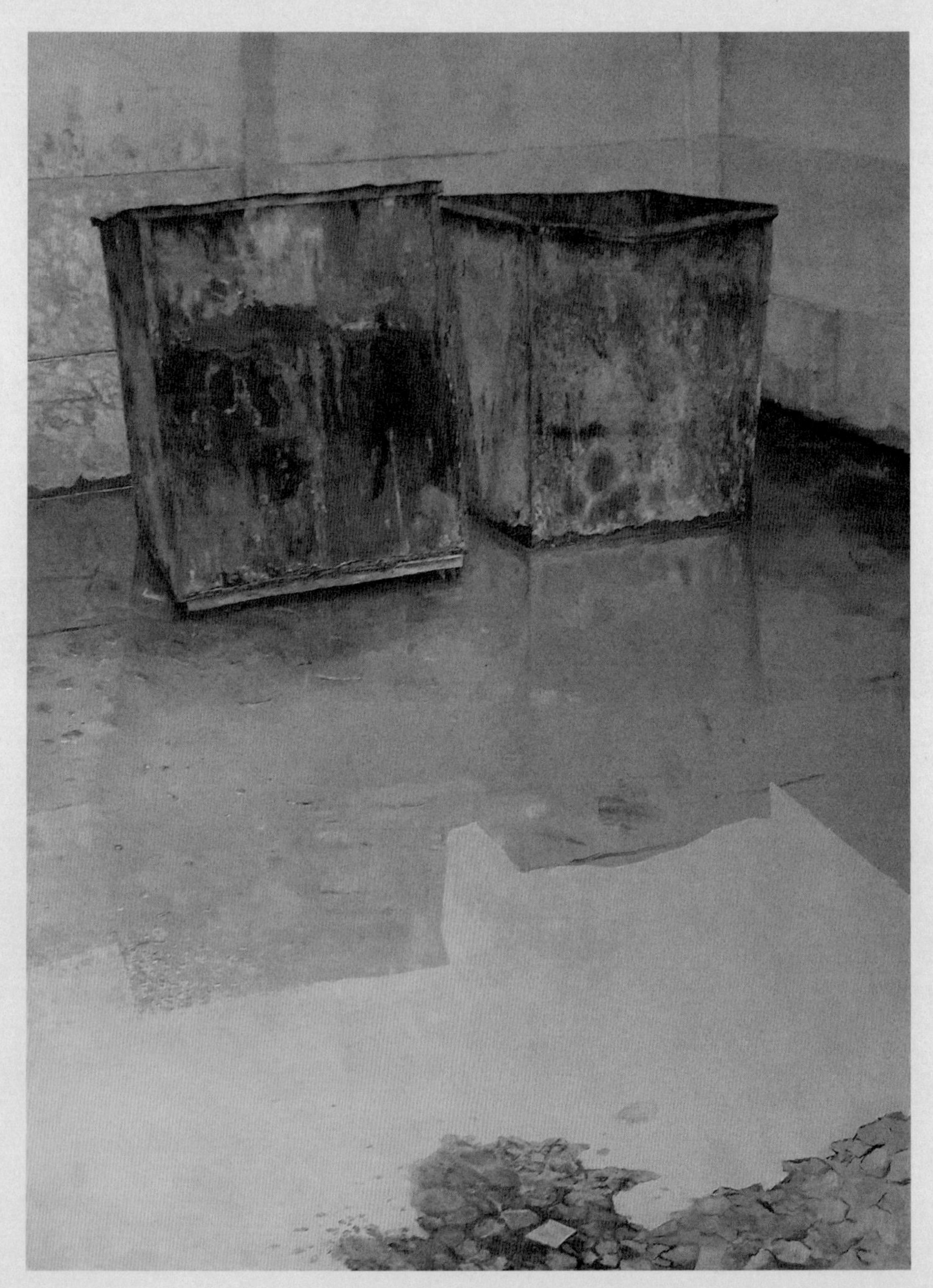

Works in Public Collections

Duolun Museum of Contemporary Arts, Shanghai
La Filature de Mulhouse
Kunstverein Bayreuth
Artothèque Strasbourg
Museum of Contemporary Arts Odessa
Archiv der Stadt Dresden
Rahmi M. Koç Fondation Istanbul
Bibliothèque Nationale de France

Books

Andrej Pirrwitz PHOTOGRAPHIE
Text Klaus Honnef: „Die Zeiten und das Bild“
Edition Braus, Heidelberg/Berlin, 2010

Andrej Pirrwitz, Piece of eternity
Catalogue, Text Philippe Piguet
Edition Galerie Schweitzer, Luxemburg, 2008

Andrej Pirrwitz, Catalogue, Text Meike Behm
Edited by Raphael12 Gallery, Frankfurt,
Gallery Lucien Schweitzer, Luxemburg,
Suty Gallery France, 2006

Andrej Pirrwitz, RBS-Untersuchungen von mehrkomponentigen Vielschichtstrukturen mit Hilfe der Computer-Simulation
Humboldt University Berlin, 1992

Bibliography

Monat der Fotografie
Fotohof Edition Salzburg, 2006, pp. 206-209

Urban Life
Catalogue Andrej Pirrwitz/Verena Guther
Edition Galerie Braunbehrens, 2008

30 Jahre Galerie von Braunbehrens
Catalogue, 2008, pp. 104-105

Fabriken Livre des artistes
Les Editions La Dragonne, Nancy, 2009

CHINA Voices
Oxfam Hong Kong, 2010, pp. 77

Mise en cène Catalogue of the private collection of Roger Castang, Perpignan, 2010, pp. 36-37

Augenweiden
Edition BRAUS Heidelberg/Berlin, 2010, pp. 15-19

30 Jahre Galerie Raphael
Edition Raphael Frankfurt, 2011, pp. 108-109

27th month of photography
Represented by Vaclav Macek, Bratislava, 2017

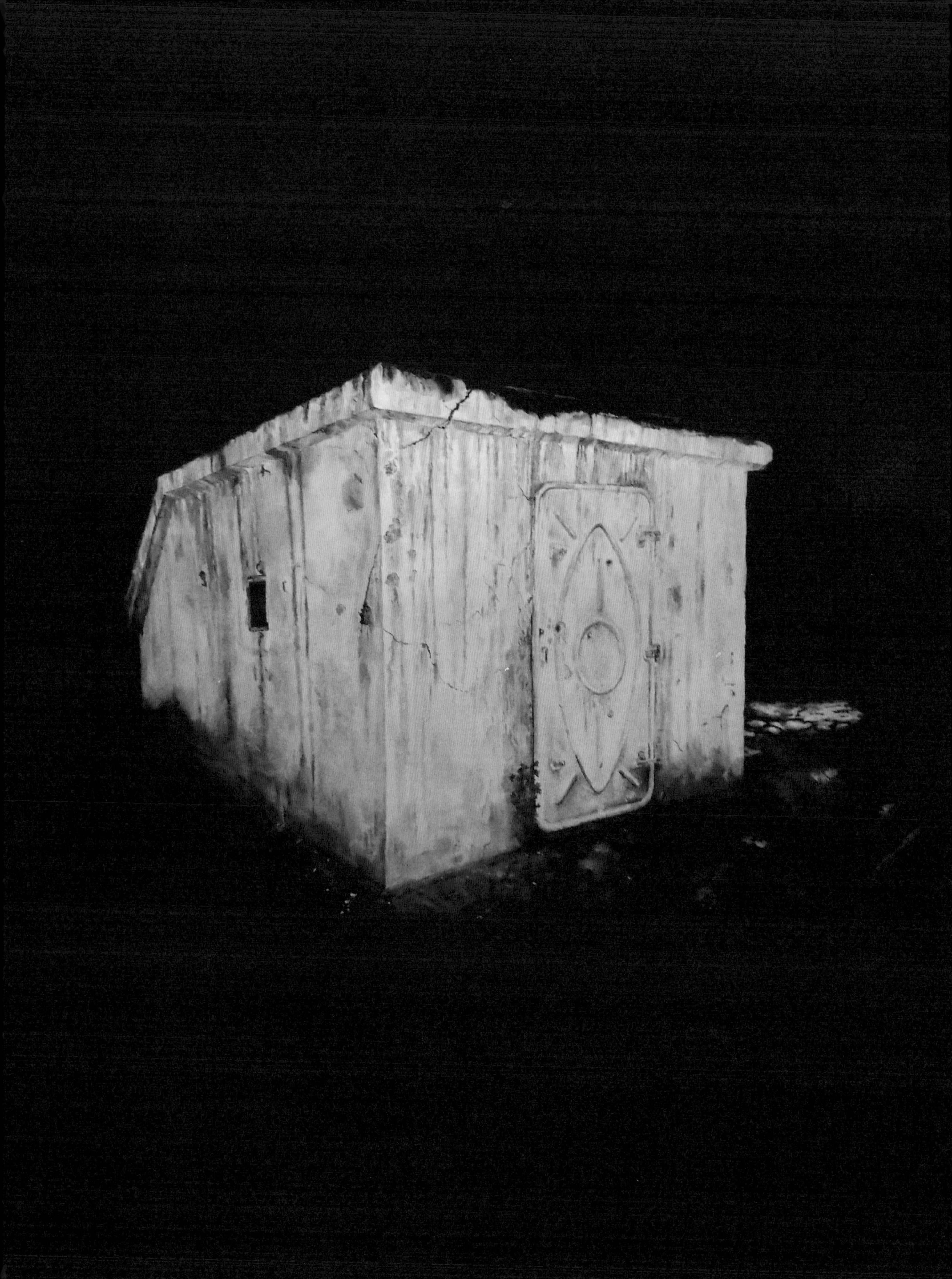

Andrej Pirrwitz wurde 1963 in Dresden geboren, wuchs in Schkopau am Fusse des mitteldeutschen Chemiekombinates Buna auf und siedelte dann nach Berlin (Ost) um, wo er auf der Mathematikspezialschule „Heinrich Hertz“ 1982 sein Abitur absolvierte.

Im selben Jahr nahm er ein Physikstudium an der Staatlichen Universität Odessa in der Ukraine auf. Die Eindrücke aus den Zeiten des Zerfalls des sowjetischen Systems am Vorabend der Perestroika, der Tschernobyl-Reaktorunfall in unmittelbarer Nachbarschaft, die Ausstrahlung des Phänomens Odessa verschmolzen mit seinen Kindheitsbildern ostdeutscher Industrielandschaft und sollten sein späteres künstlerisches Schaffen wie ein roter Faden durchwirken.

Nach Beendigung seiner wissenschaftlichen Laufbahn 1992 mit einer Promotion über Ionenstrahlverfahren in der Festkörperphysik an der Humbold-Universität zu Berlin entschied er, ins Herz des Kapitalismus vorzudringen und begann als Manager des amerikanischen Industriekonzerns Eaton in dessen Zentrale in Strasbourg. Er ließ nicht nur Familie, Heim, Wissenschaft und Sprache hinter sich, er begab sich auf einen Pilgerweg, der zwischen den Gesellschaftsordnungen oszillierte: sein Arbeitsgebiet umfasste einerseits die modernen Produktionsstätten Eatons in Westdeutschland, Italien, Frankreich, den USA und andererseits die Kombinate in Polen, Russland, auf dem Balkan und in Ostdeutschland. Zu großen Teilen stillgelegt, noch nach kommunistischem Muster organisiert, gewährten sie ihm solche Art von Räumen, deren Stille er von jeher suchte.

Neun Jahre später, 2001, beendete er das Experiment abrupt, erlernte die Fotografie mit der 4x5 Linhoff Großbildkamera und suchte sich fortan seine Zonen stehengebliebener Zeit als freischaffender Künstler, fotografierend und malend, mit Wohnsitz in Strasbourg und einem Atelier in Berlin.

Stationen seiner künstlerischen Laufbahn waren Arbeitsaufenthalte in Nordchina und Hong Kong (im Rahmen des Kunstförderprogramms des Centre européen d'actions artistiques in Strasbourg), eine Residenz an der Filature de Mulhouse sowie Dozententätigkeiten im Bereich Fotografie an der Lu Xun Academy of Fine Arts in Shenyang sowie an der Hochschule für Kunst in Mulhouse „Le Quai“ und während der Dresdner Sommerakademie für Kunst. Seine Arbeiten wurden in über 60 Einzelausstellungen in Galerien, Kunstvereinen und Museen in Europa, den USA, China und der Ukraine gezeigt.

Andrej Pirrwitz naît à Dresde en 1963 et grandit à Schkopau, en Allemagne centrale, au pied du combinat chimique Buna, avant que sa famille ne déménage à Berlin-Est, où il obtiendra son baccalauréat du lycée spécial de mathématiques Heinrich-Hertz en 1982.

La même année, il commence à étudier la physique à l'Université d'État d'Odessa en Ukraine. Plus tard, ses impressions de l'effondrement de l'Union soviétique à l'aube de la perestroïka, de la catastrophe nucléaire de Tchernobyl et du charme singulier d'Odessa allaient se confondre avec ses souvenirs d'enfance des paysages industriels est-allemands pour former le fil rouge qui traverse son œuvre.

Après avoir complété son cursus académique en 1992 par un doctorat sur les techniques des faisceaux d'ions en physique du solide à l'Université Humboldt de Berlin, il décide de pénétrer au cœur du capitalisme en acceptant un poste de manager au siège strasbourgeois de la société américaine Eaton. Laissant derrière lui famille, maison, science et langue, il s'embarque dans un périple qui l'amène à faire la navette entre deux modèles de société contrastés, sa zone d'intervention comprenant les usines modernes de l'entreprise en Allemagne de l'Ouest, en Italie, en France et aux États-Unis, mais aussi les combinats en Pologne, Russie, dans les Balkans et en Allemagne de l'Est. Ces installations en partie désaffectées, fonctionnant encore selon des principes communistes, présentent le genre d'espaces dont le silence l'a de tout temps attiré.

Neuf ans plus tard, en 2001, il termine abruptement l'expérience et apprend la photographie avec une chambre grand format Linhoff 4x5. Depuis, il part à la recherche de lieux où le temps s'est arrêté, qu'il documente en tant qu'artiste, photographe et peintre vivant à Strasbourg et travaillant depuis son atelier à Berlin.

Pour ses recherches, il a séjourné dans le nord de la Chine et à Hong Kong (dans le cadre du programme de bourses du Centre européen d'actions artistiques à Strasbourg) et a effectué une résidence à La Filature à Mulhouse. Il a par ailleurs enseigné aux départements de photographie de l'Académie des beaux-arts Lu Xun à Shenyang et du Quai, école supérieure d'art de Mulhouse ainsi qu'à l'Académie d'été des arts visuels de Dresde. Son travail a fait l'objet de plus de soixante expositions personnelles dans des galeries, centres d'art et musées en Europe, en Amérique, en Chine et en Ukraine.

Biography

Andrej Pirrwitz was born in Dresden in 1963 and grew up in Schkopau, Central Germany, at the foot of the chemical combine Buna, before his family moved to East Berlin, where he graduated from the Heinrich Hertz special mathematics high school in 1982.

That same year he began studying physics at Odessa State University in Ukraine. His impressions of the collapse of the Soviet Union on the eve of perestroika, the nearby Chernobyl nuclear disaster and the peculiar charm of Odessa would later merge with his childhood memories of East German industrial landscapes to form the red thread running through his artistic work.

After completing his academic curriculum in 1992 with a PhD on ion-beam techniques in solid-state physics at Humboldt University in Berlin, he decided to penetrate into the heart of capitalism and took up a managerial position at the Strasbourg headquarters of the US corporation Eaton. Leaving behind family, home, science and language, he embarked on a journey that saw him travelling back and forth between contrasting social orders, his area of responsibility including the company's modern production facilities in West Germany, Italy, France and the USA, but also the combines in Poland, Russia, the Balkans and East Germany. These partly decommissioned facilities, still functioning according to communist principles, featured the kind of spaces whose silence he had always yearned for.

Nine years later, in 2001, he ended the experiment abruptly and studied photography working with a large-format Linhoff 4x5 camera. Ever since, he has been exploring places where time stands still as a freelance artist, photographer and painter living in Strasbourg and working from his studio in Berlin.

As part of his research, he has travelled to northern China and Hong Kong (in the framework of the bursary programme of the Centre européen d'actions artistiques in Strasbourg) and completed a residency at La Filature in Mulhouse. He has lectured in the photography departments of the Lu Xun Academy of Fine Arts in Shenyang and Le Quai, école supérieure d'art in Mulhouse as well as at the Dresden Summer Academy for Visual Arts. His work has been presented in more than sixty solo exhibitions in galleries, art centres and museums in Europe, America, China and Ukraine.

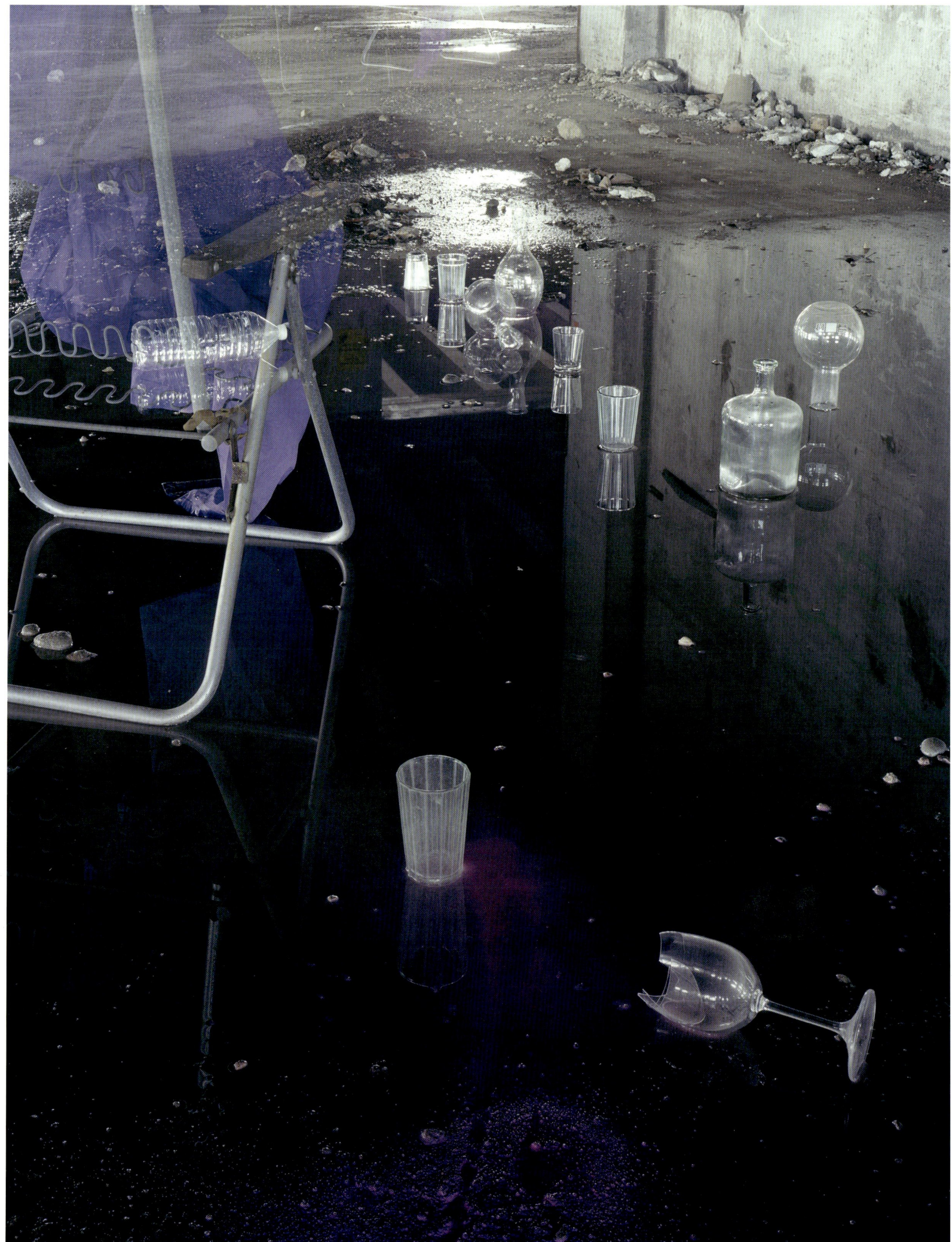

Schach-matt II, 2020

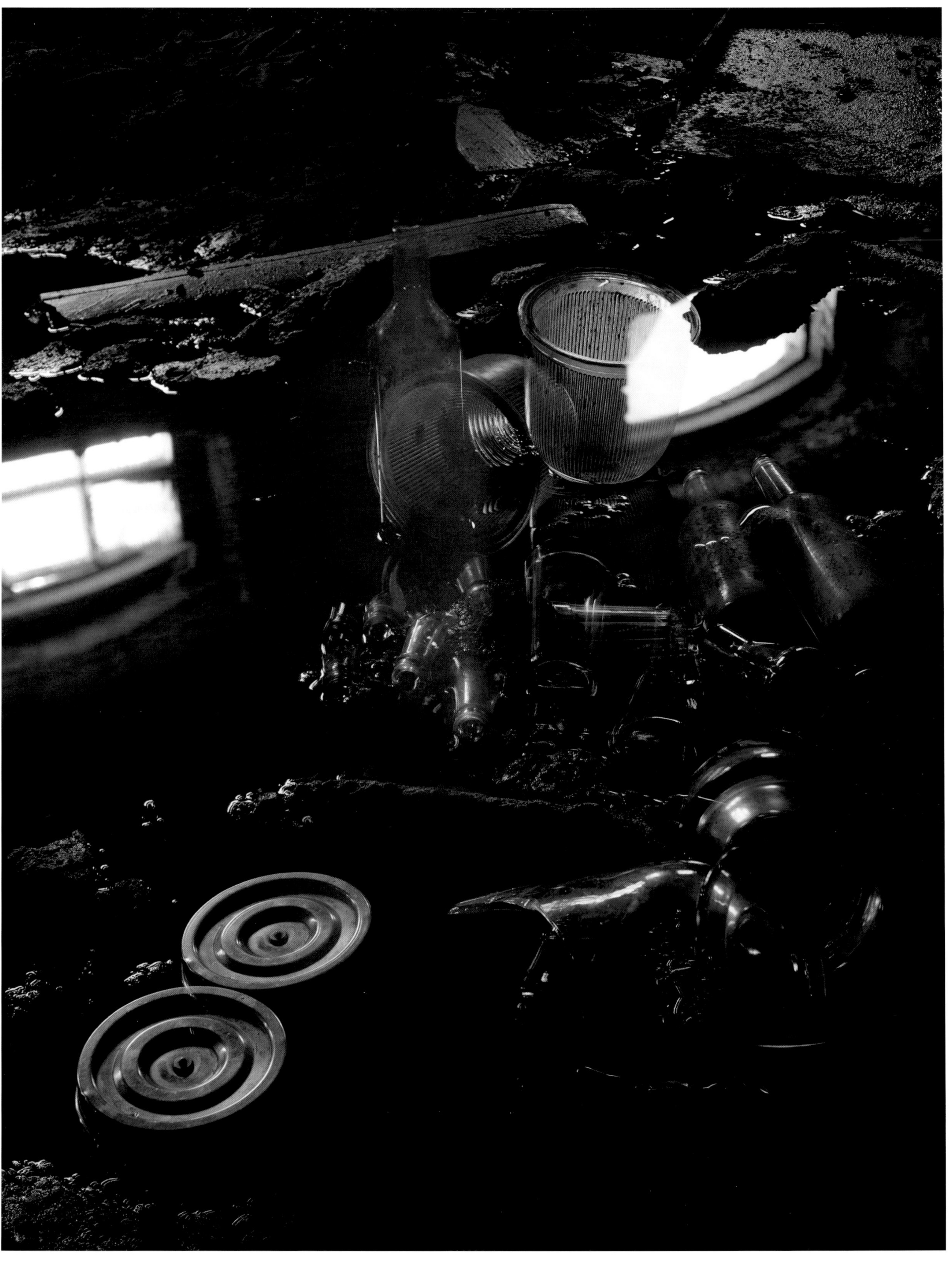

nature morte II, 2020

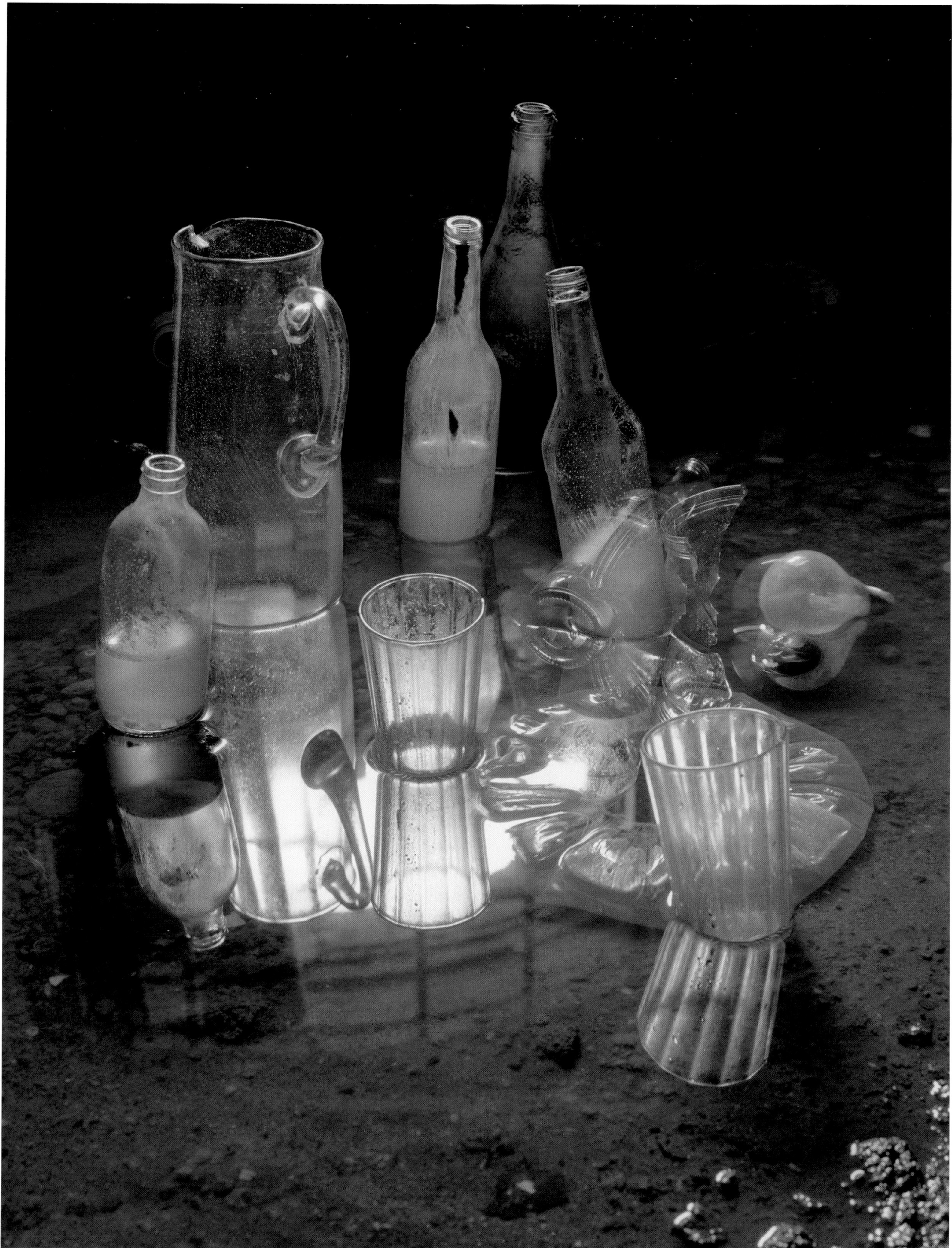

nature morte I, 2013

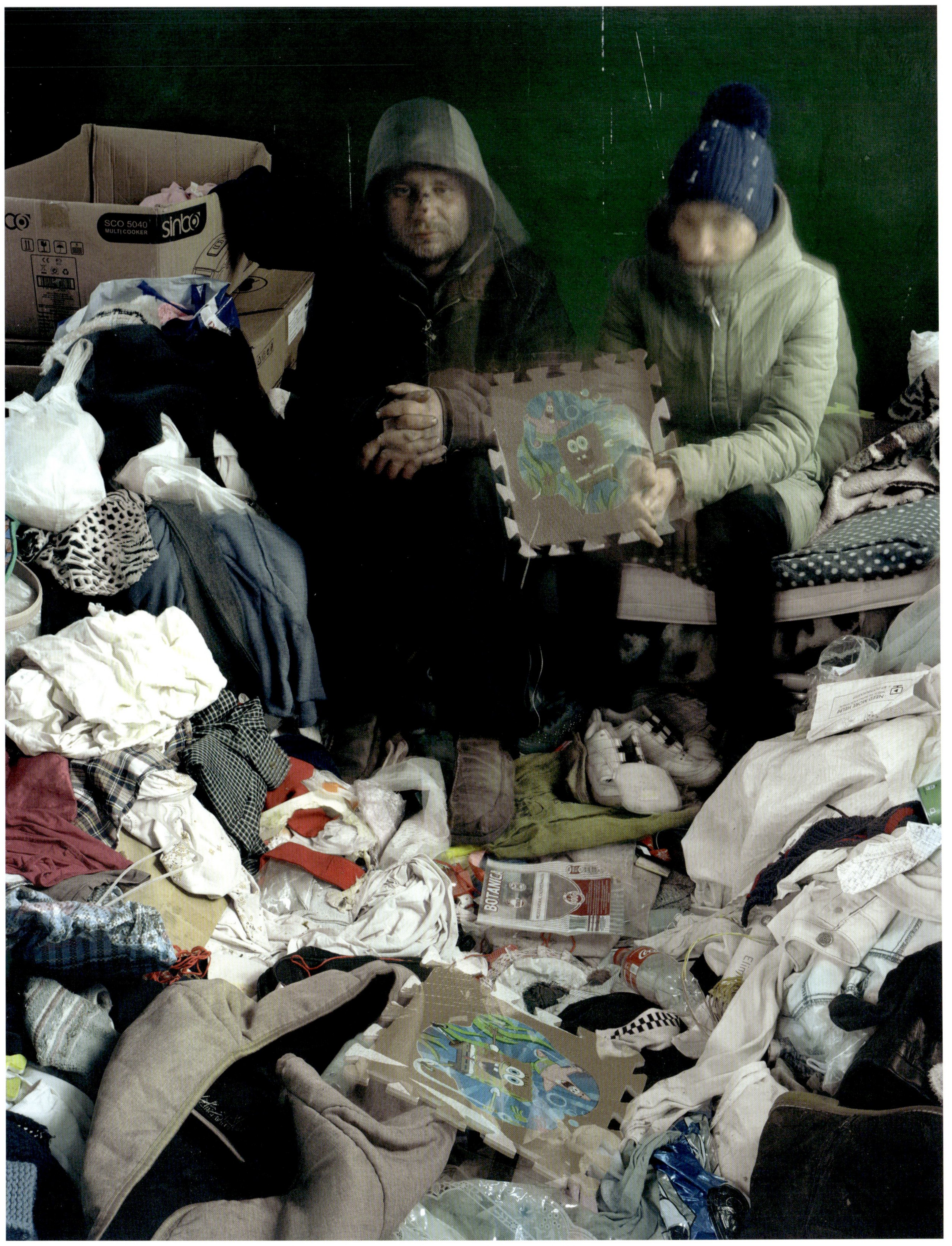

sitzendes Paar, 2019

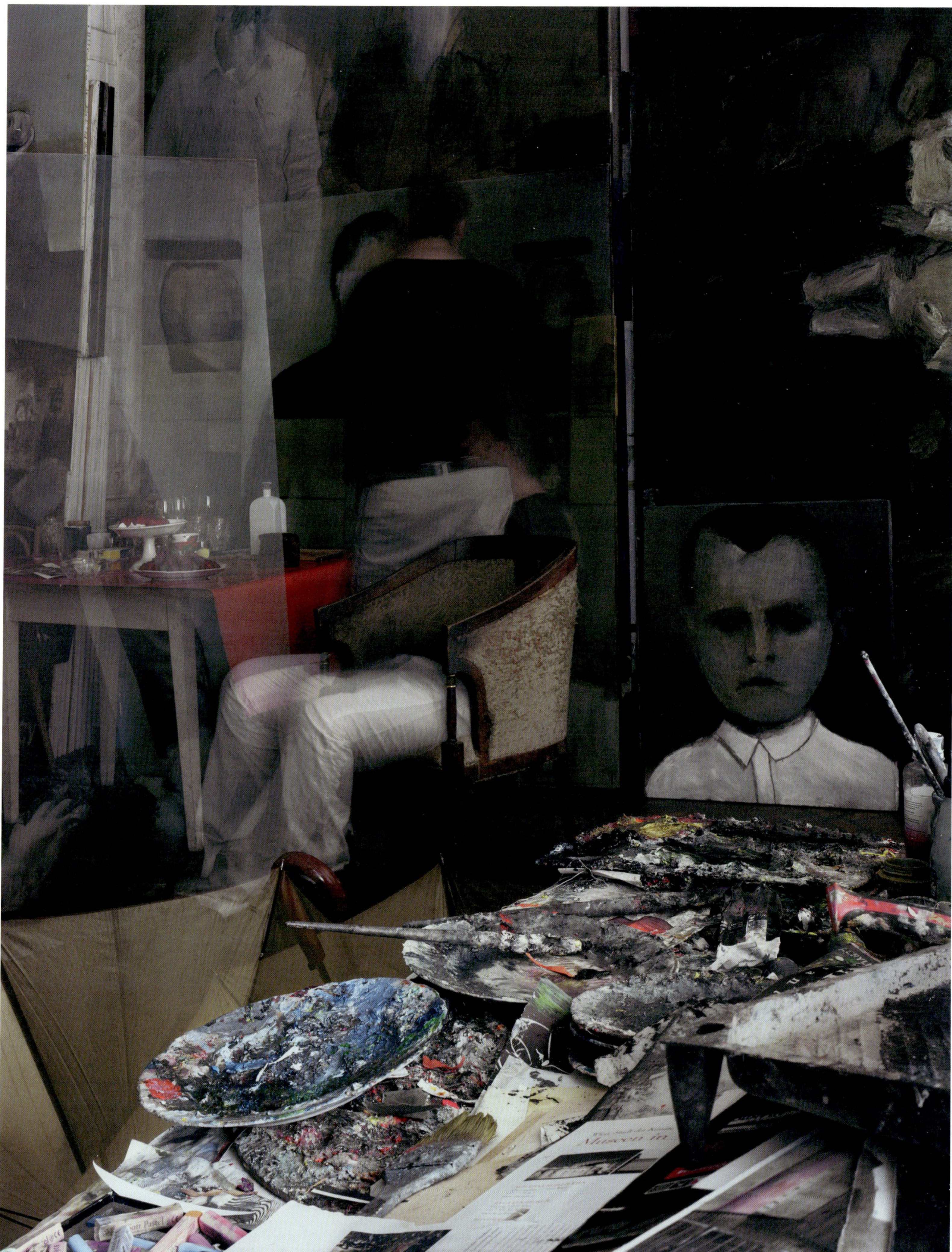

Pizzastube, 2013

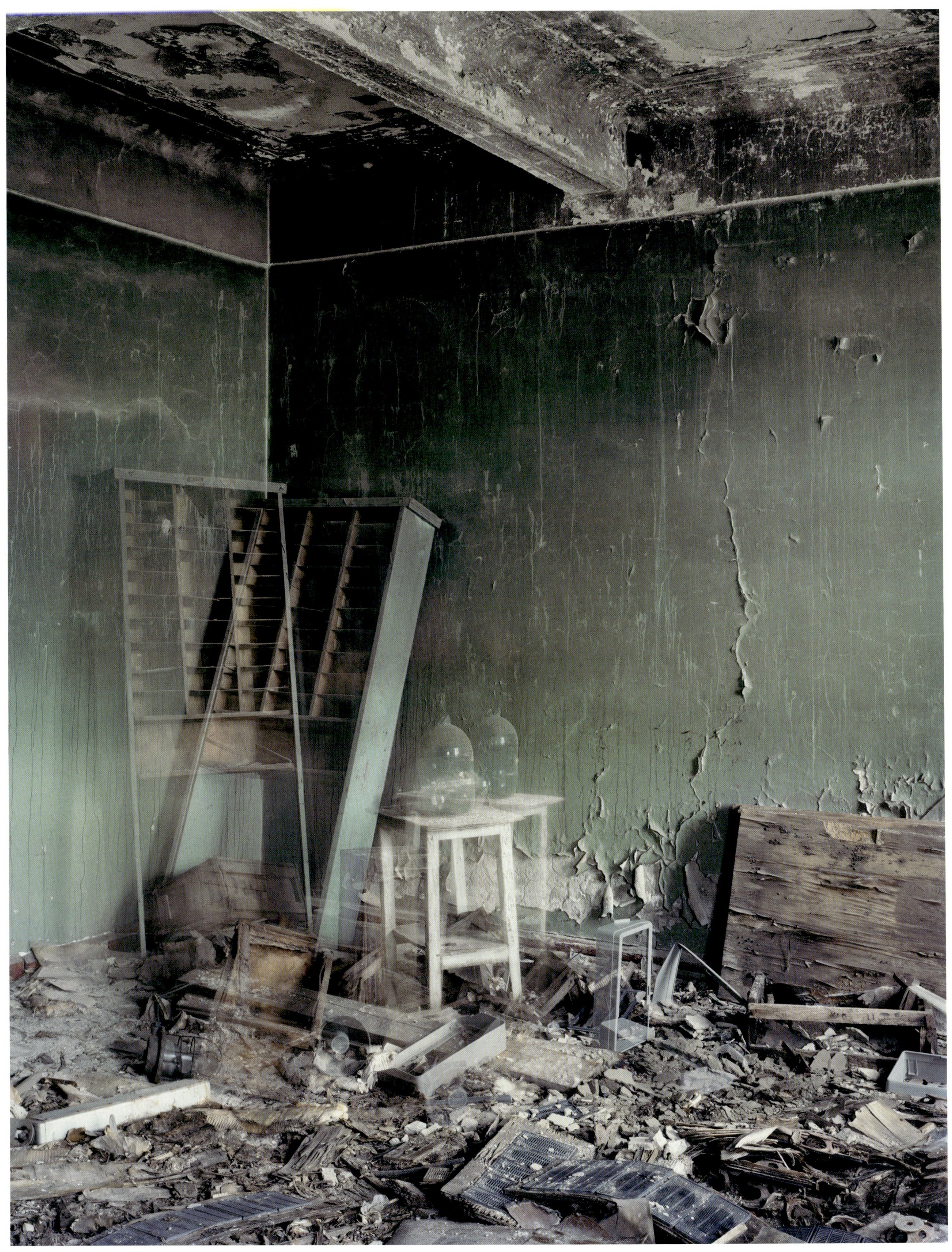

Kassetten-Korner, 2018

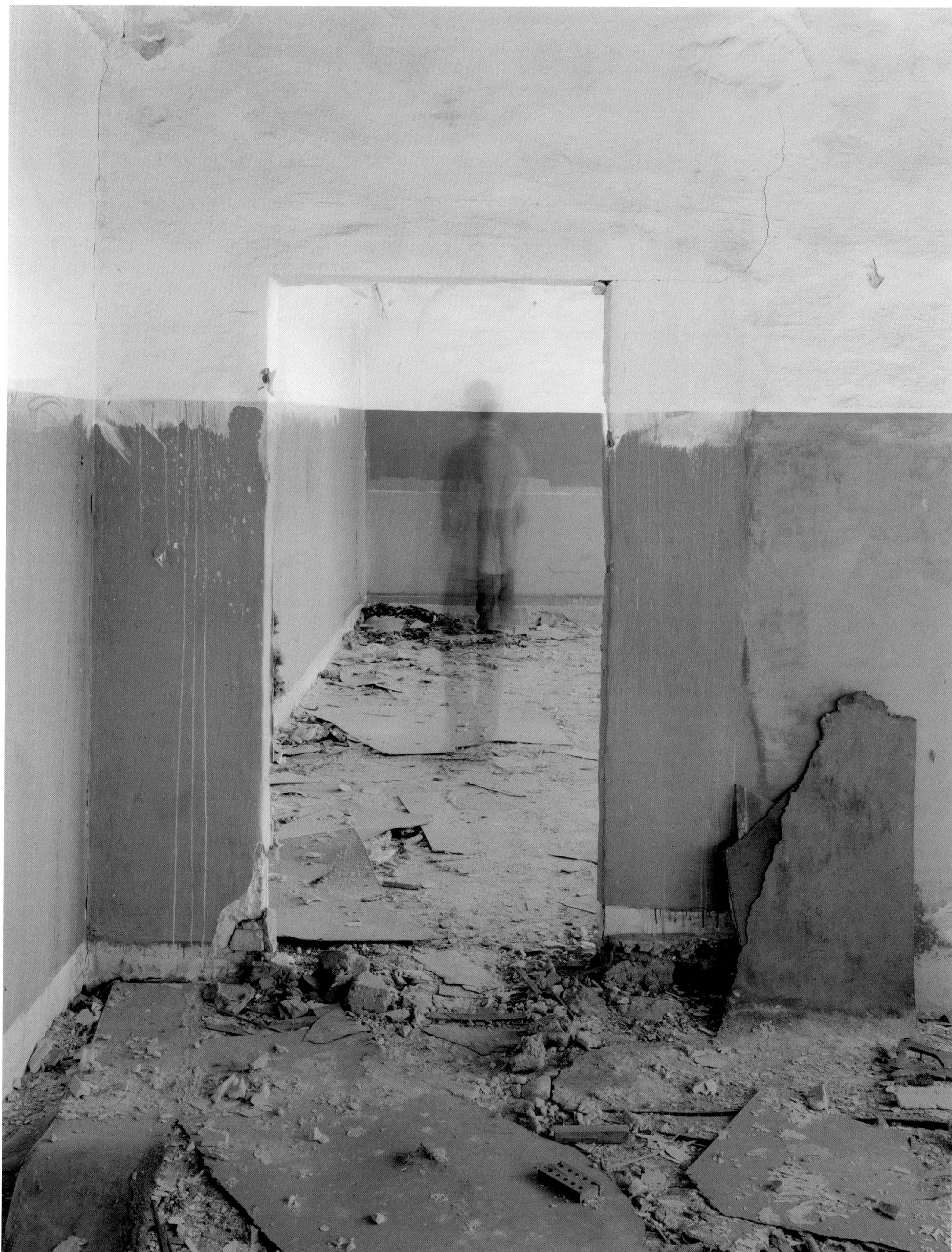

mise au green, 2016

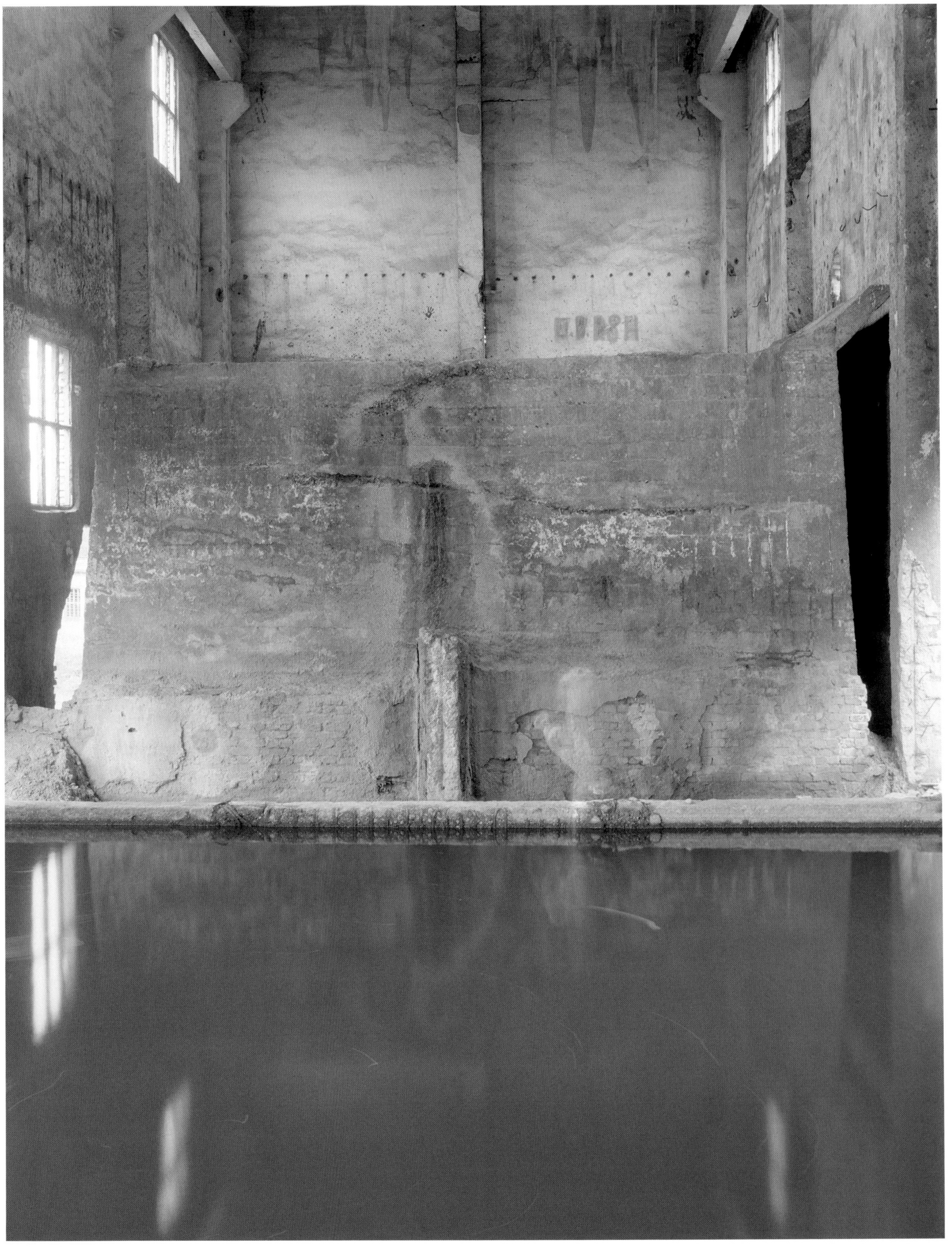

chateau d'eau, 2016

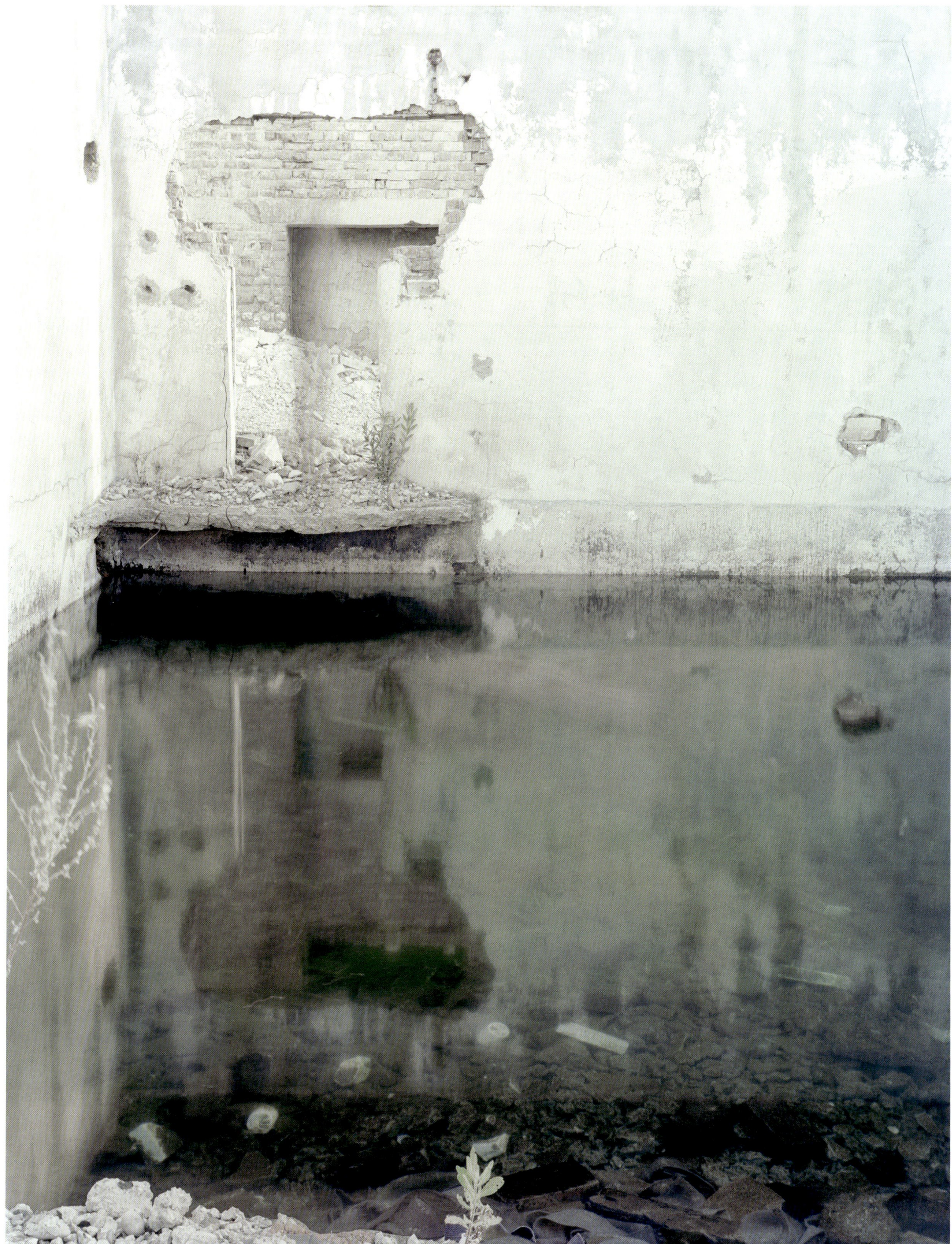

E-lake, 2016

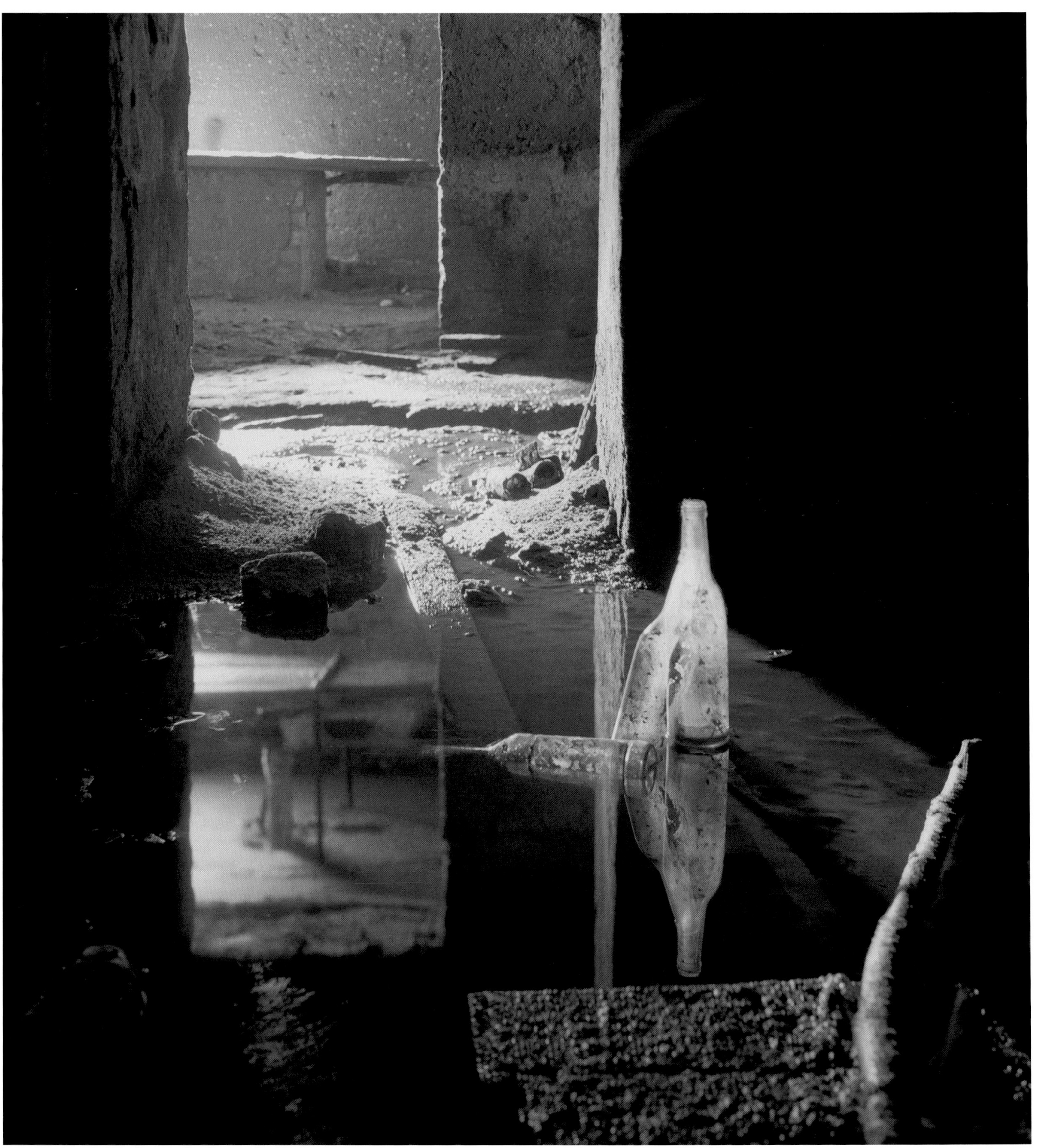

Schiffe versenken I, 2014 (detail)

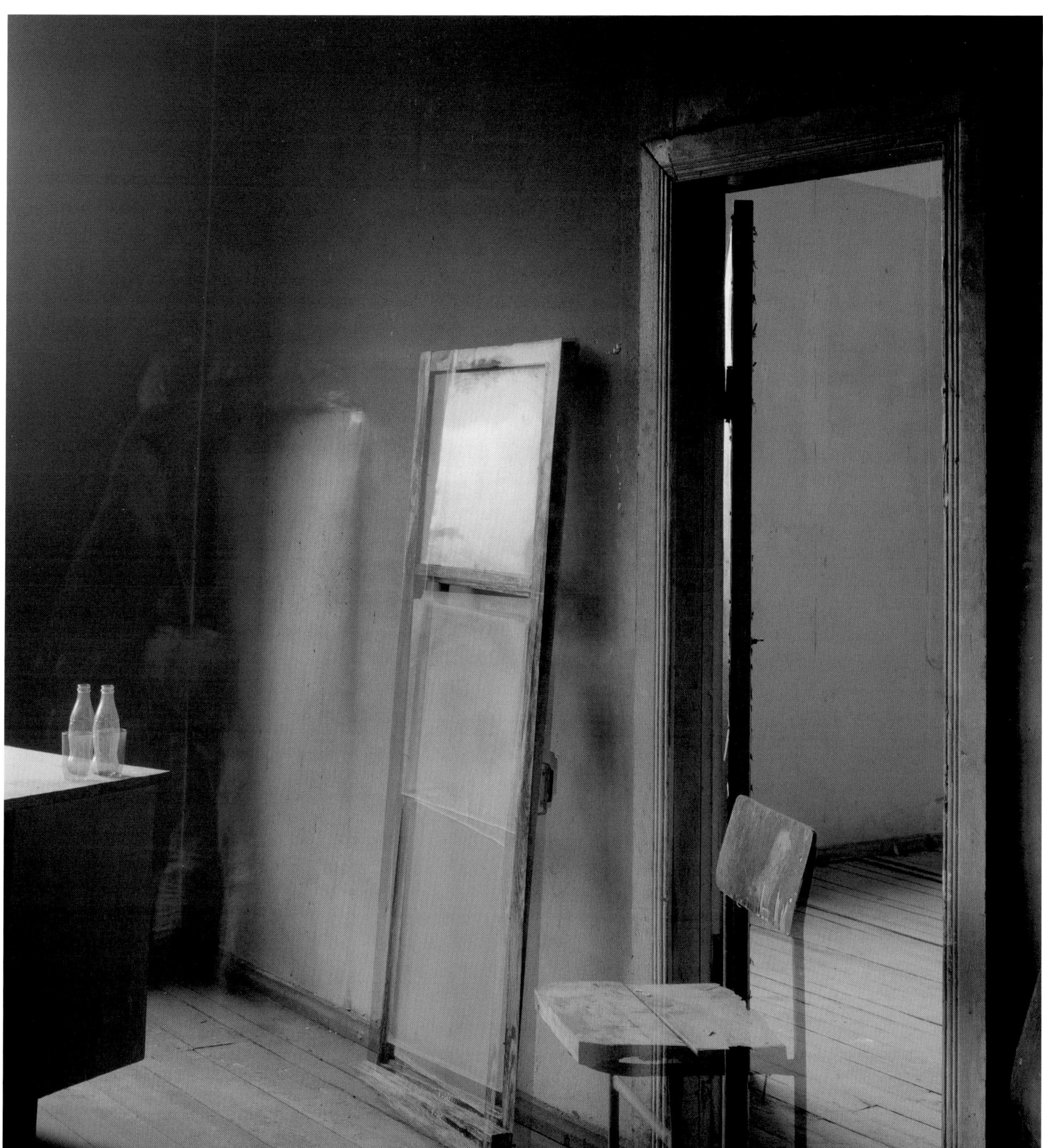

Heimlichkeiten, 2019

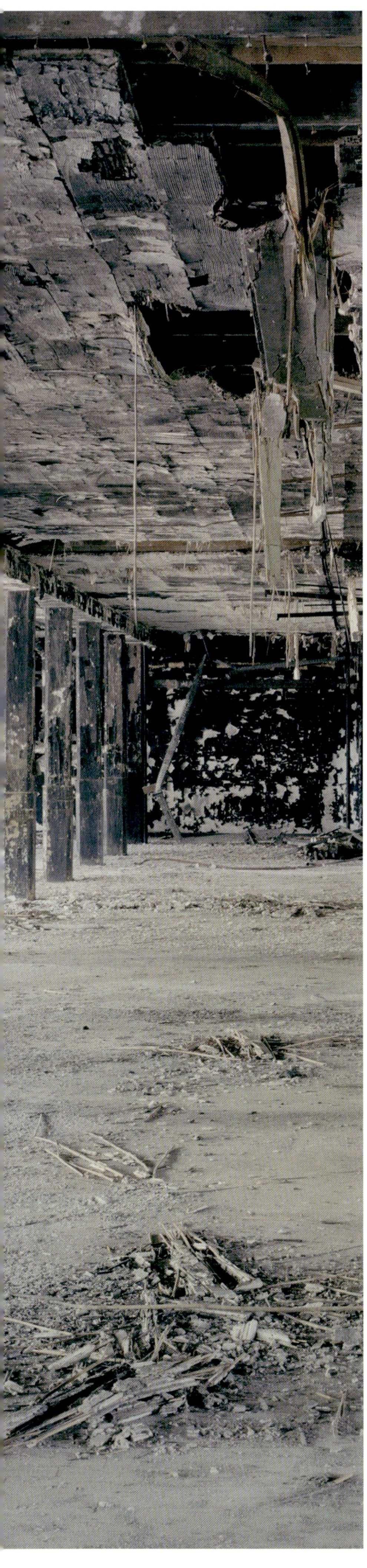

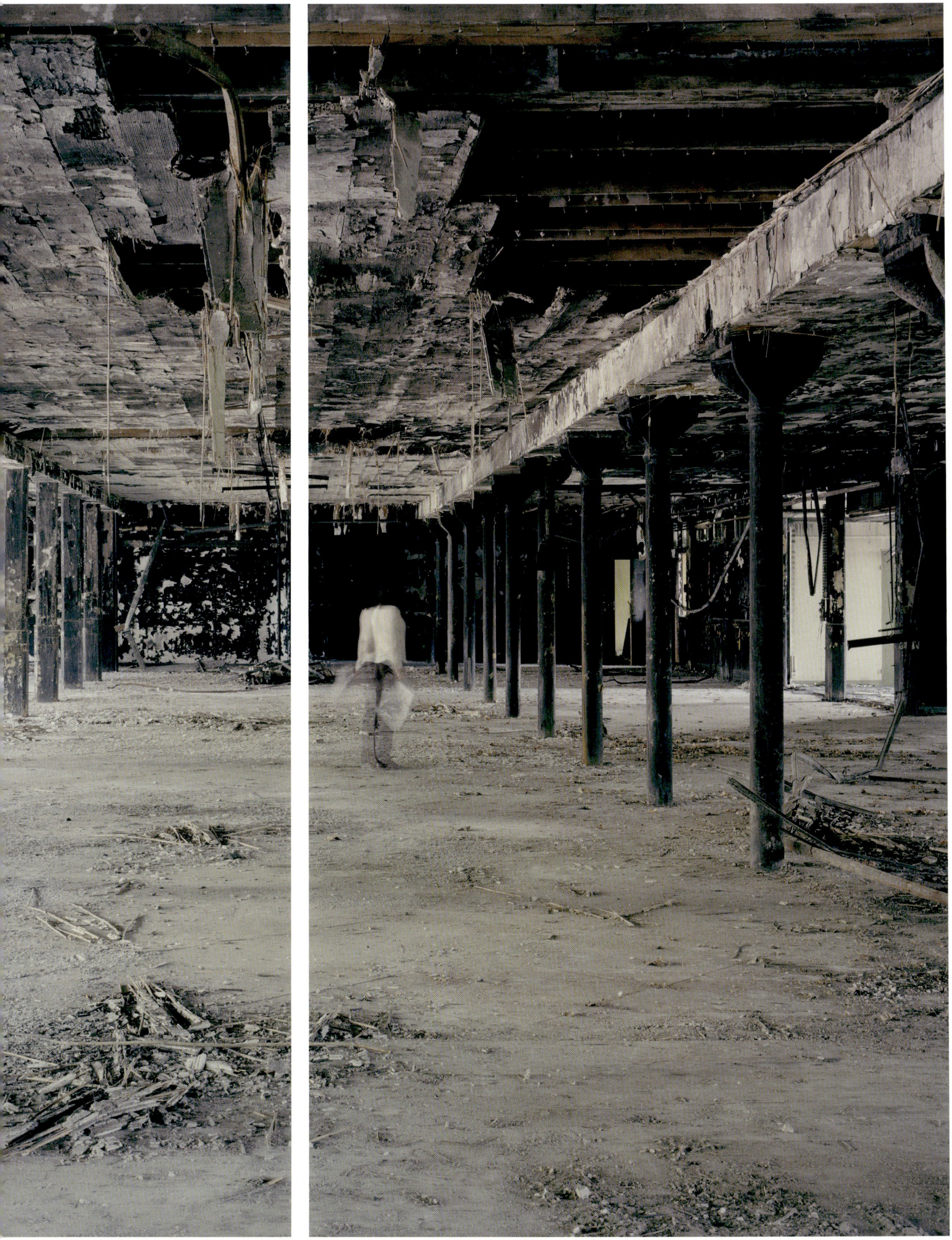

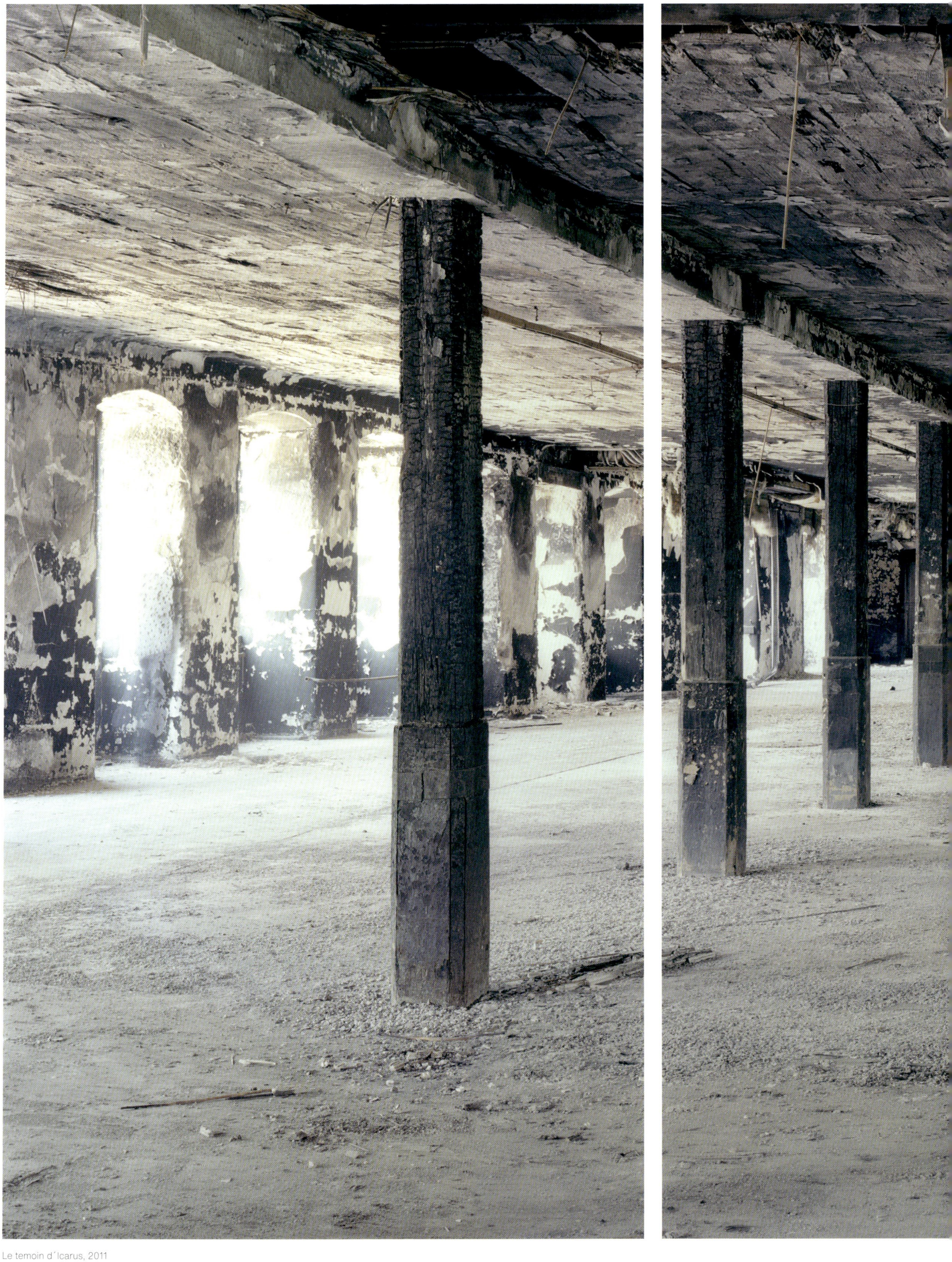

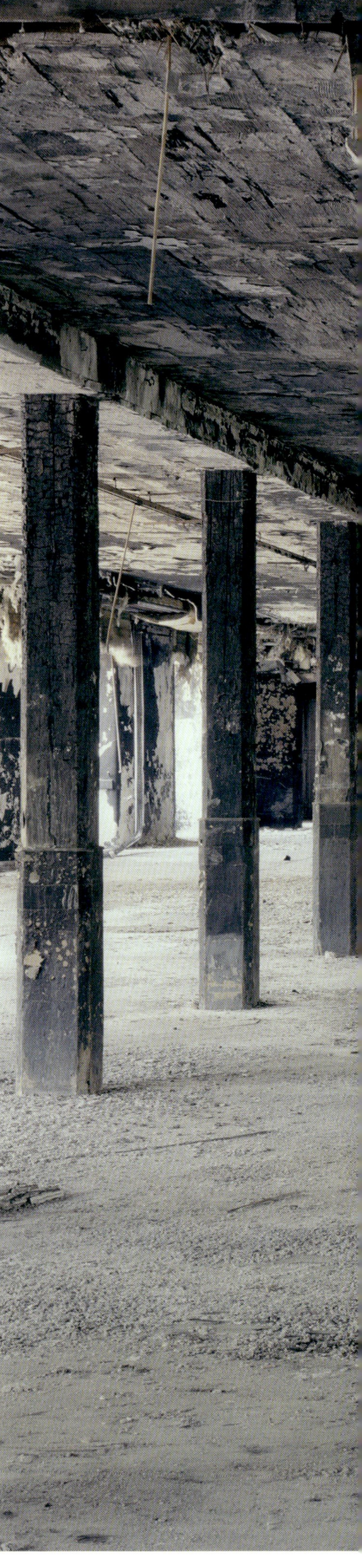

Le temoin d´Icarus, 2011

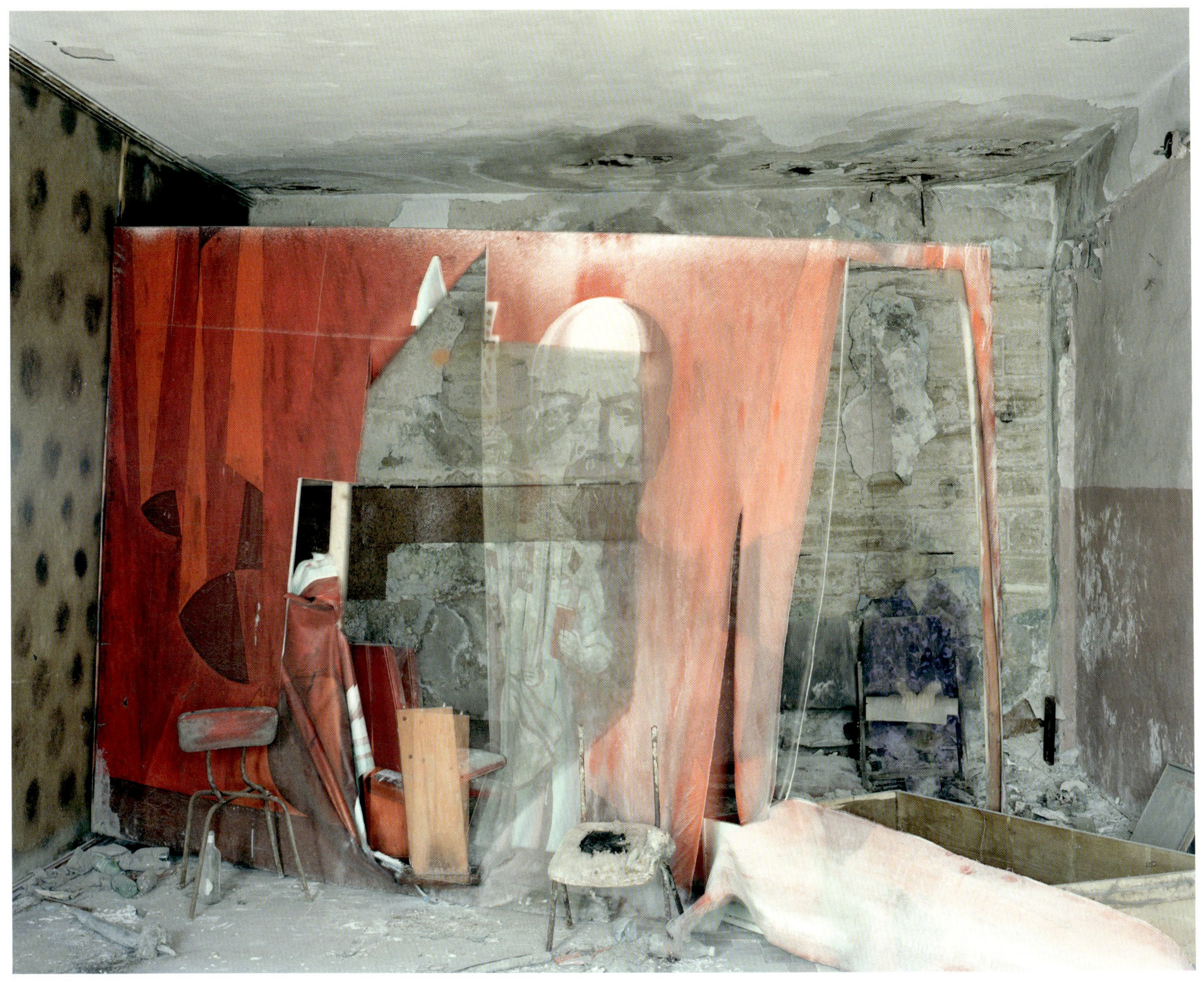

good bye Lenin, 2012

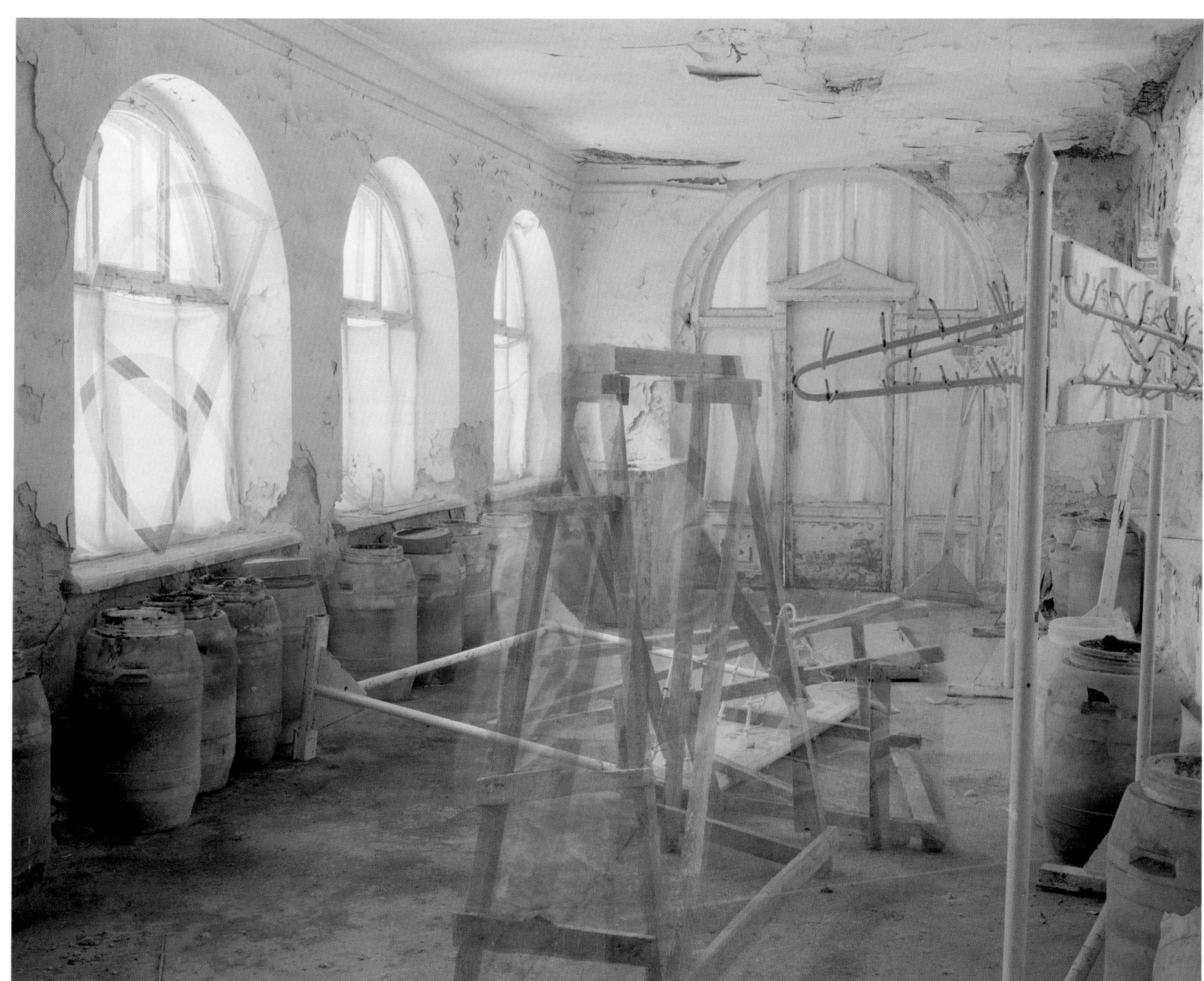
wardrobe pusher II, 2014

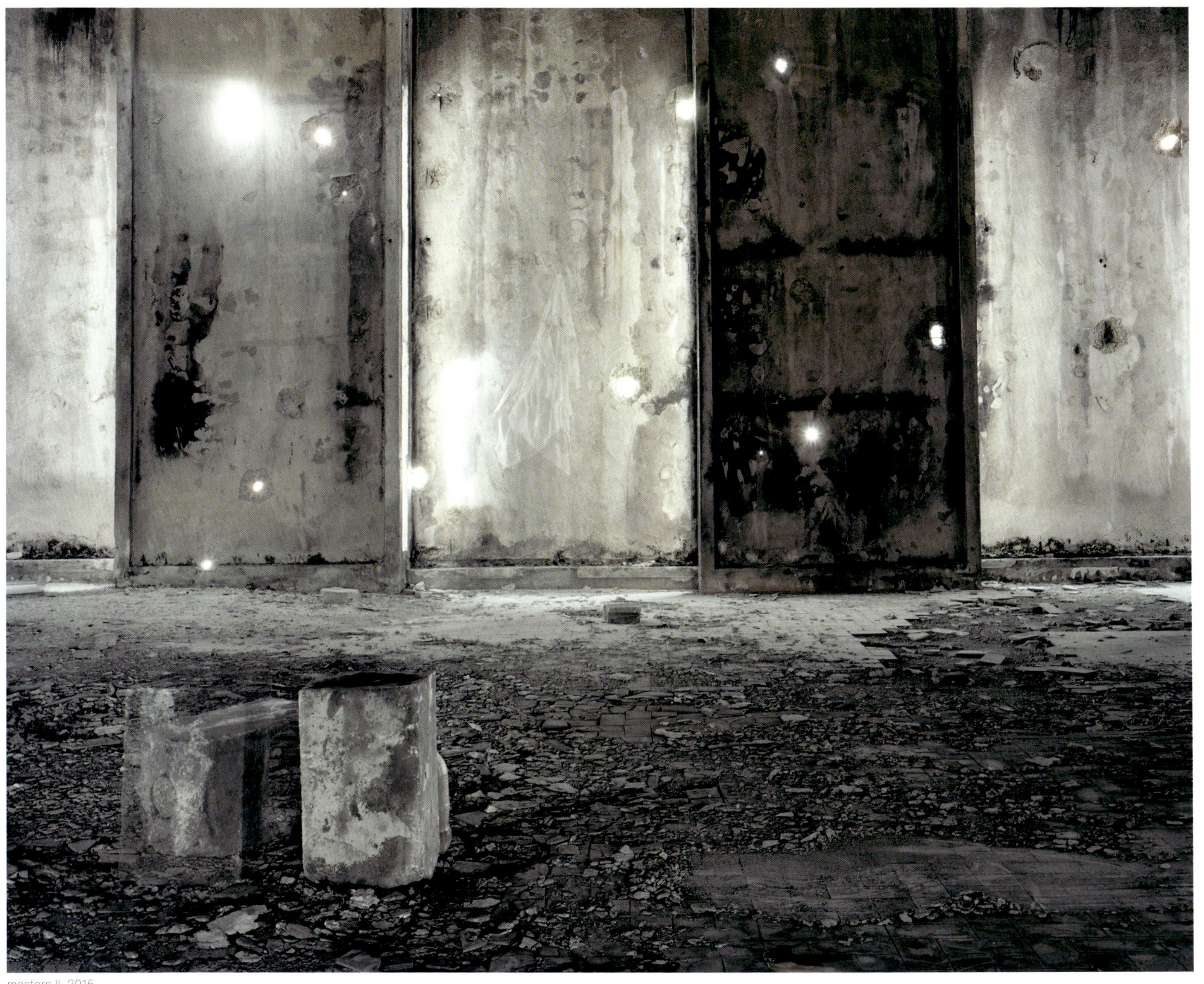

mostars II, 2015

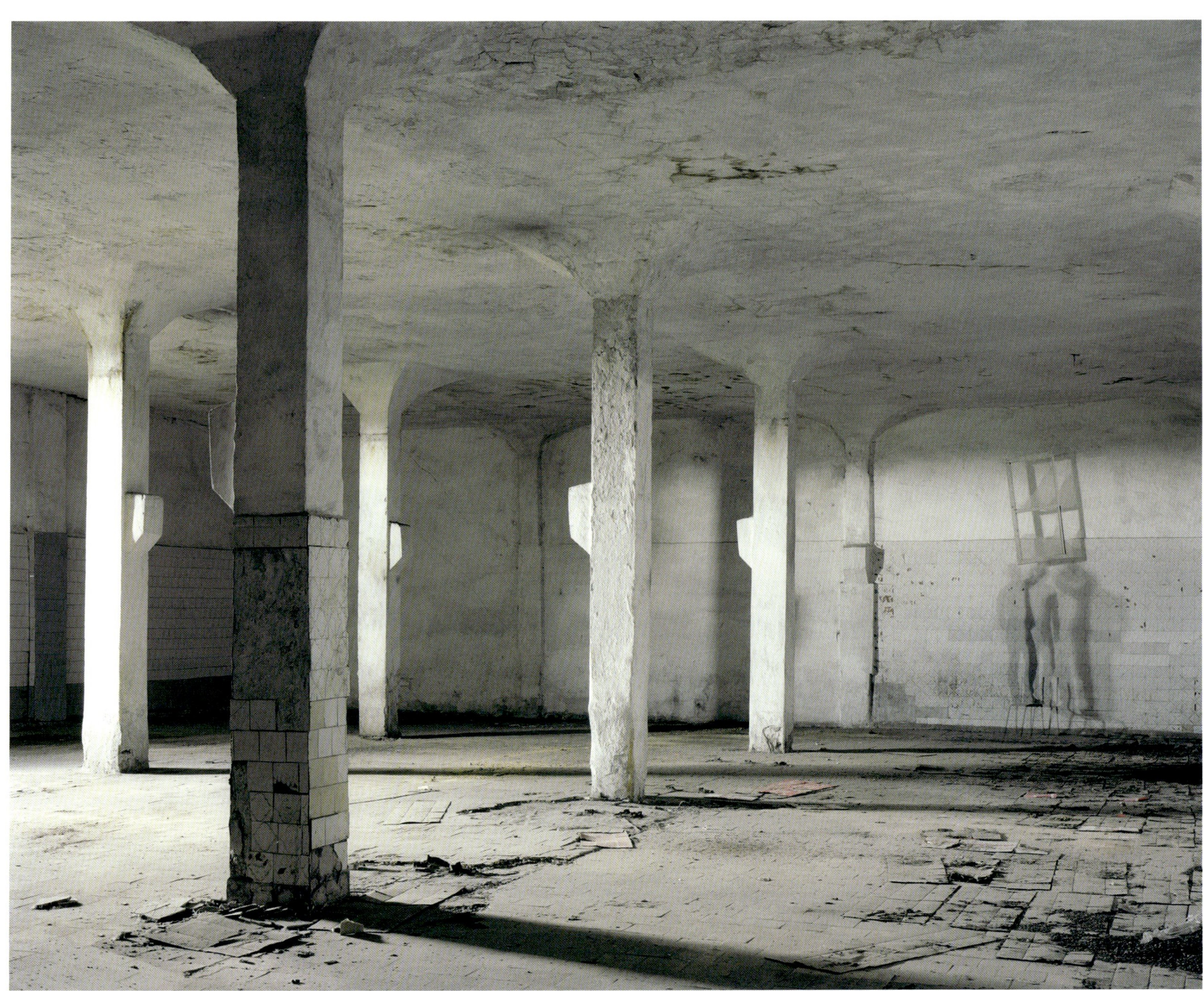

Stille Krönung, 2012

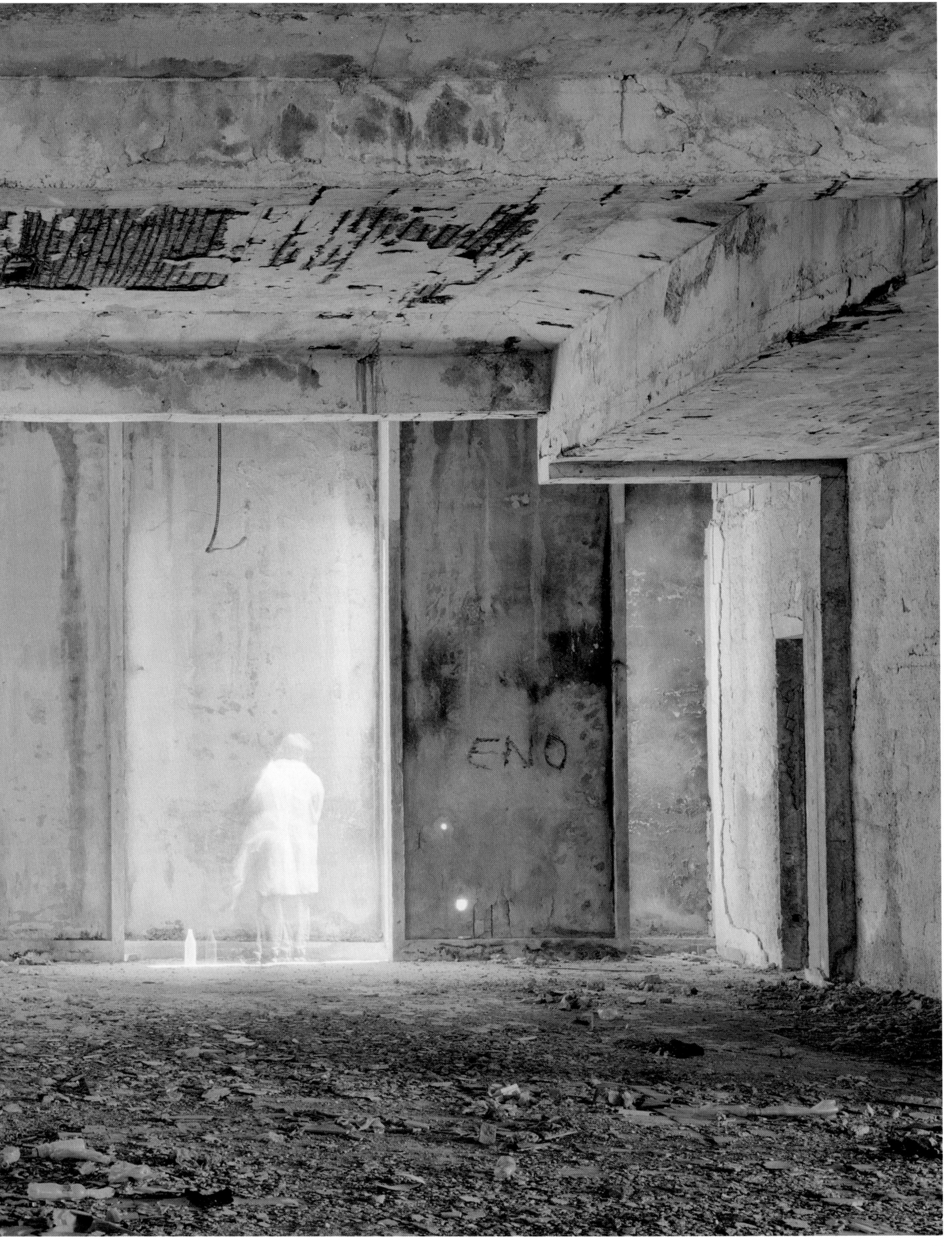
ENO

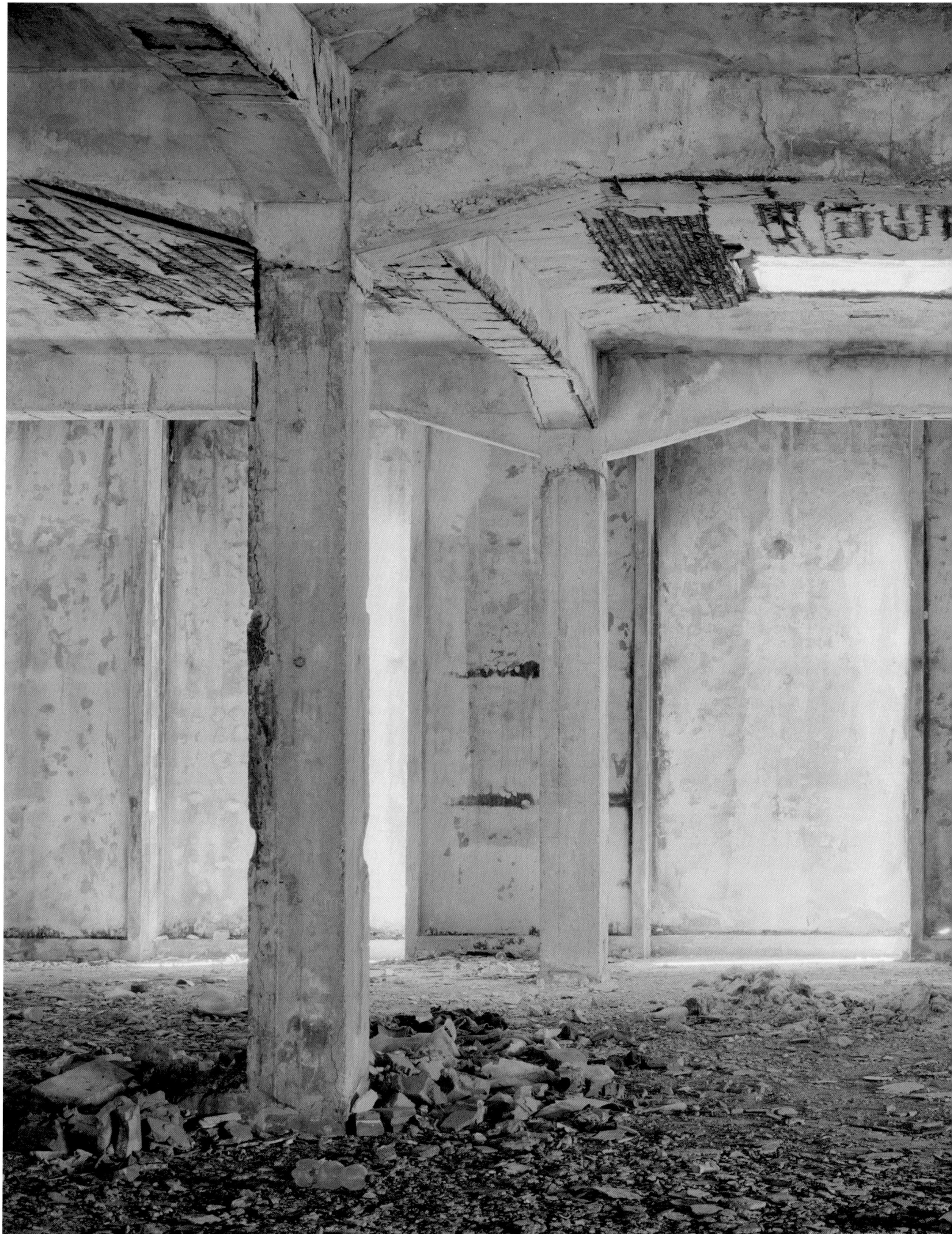

mostars I, 2015

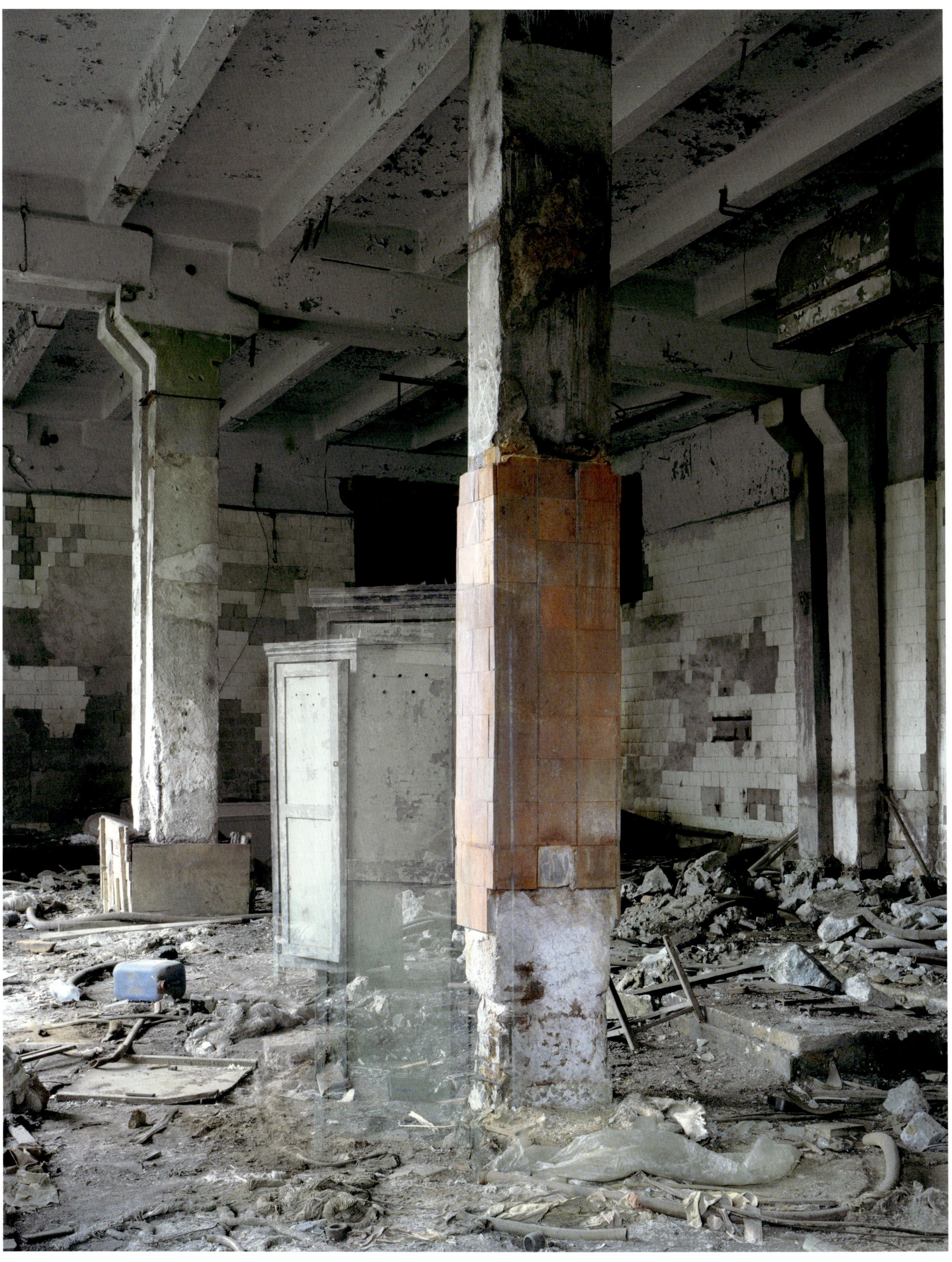

quadrature en rose, 2019

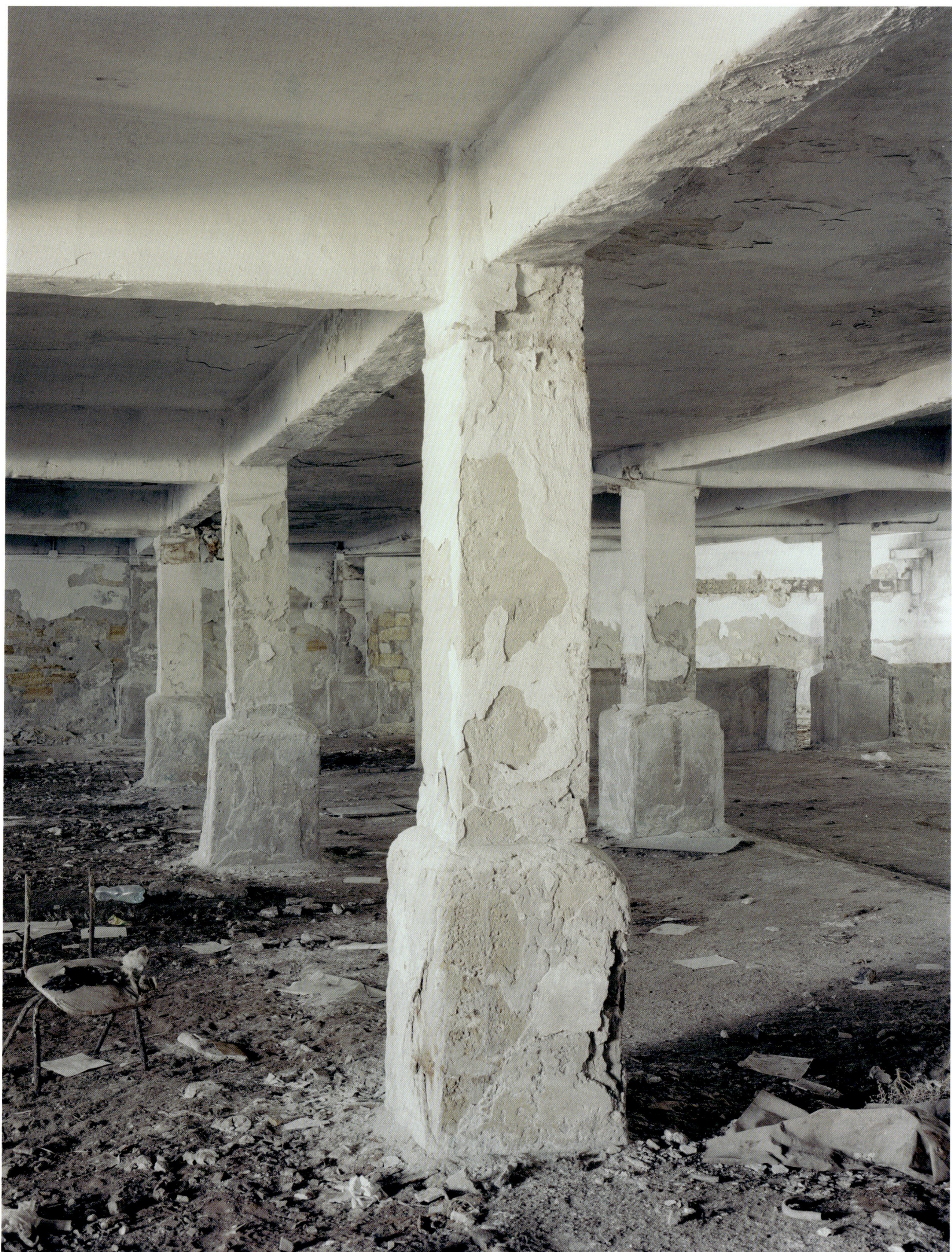

erstarrte Bresche, 2012

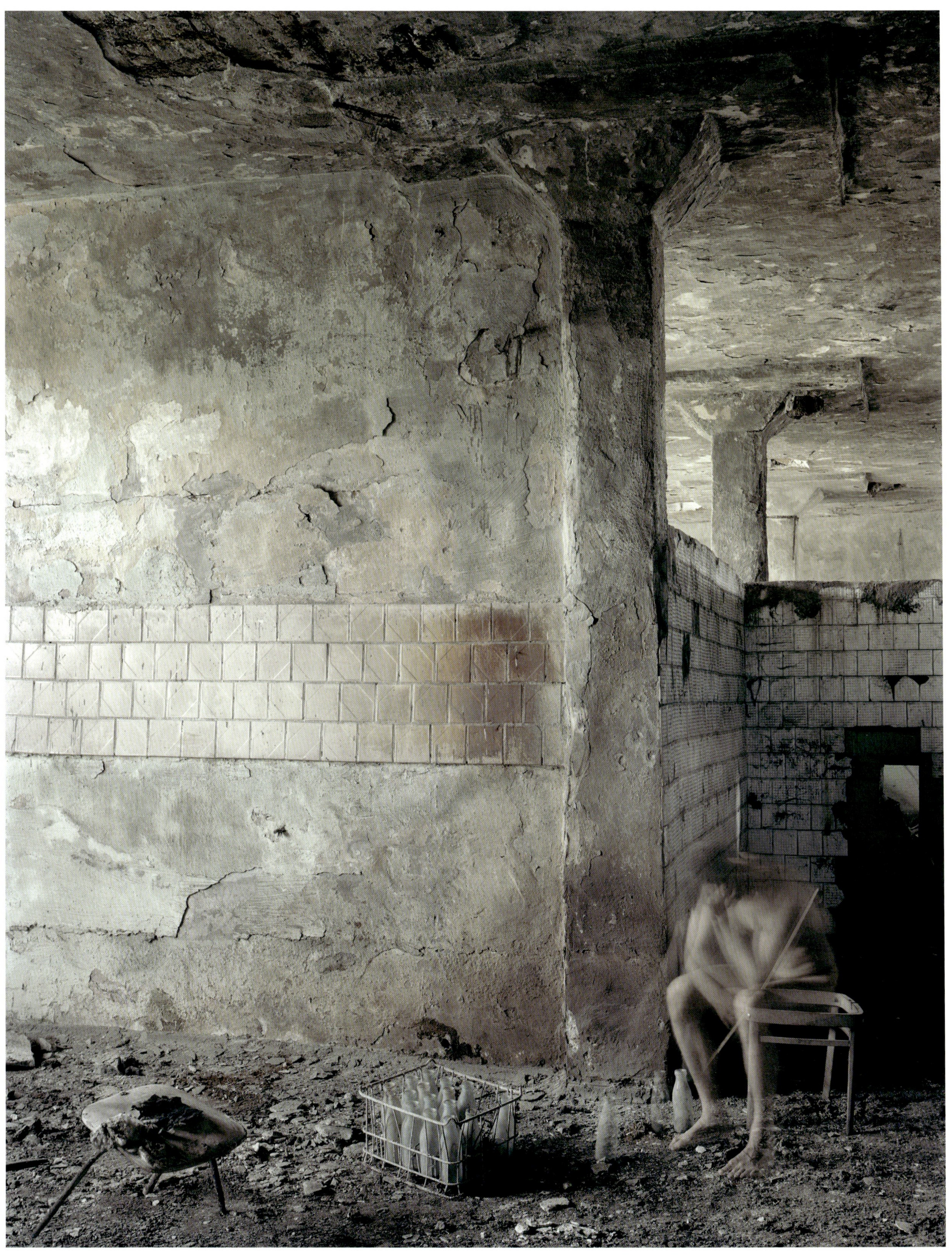

moloko I, 2012

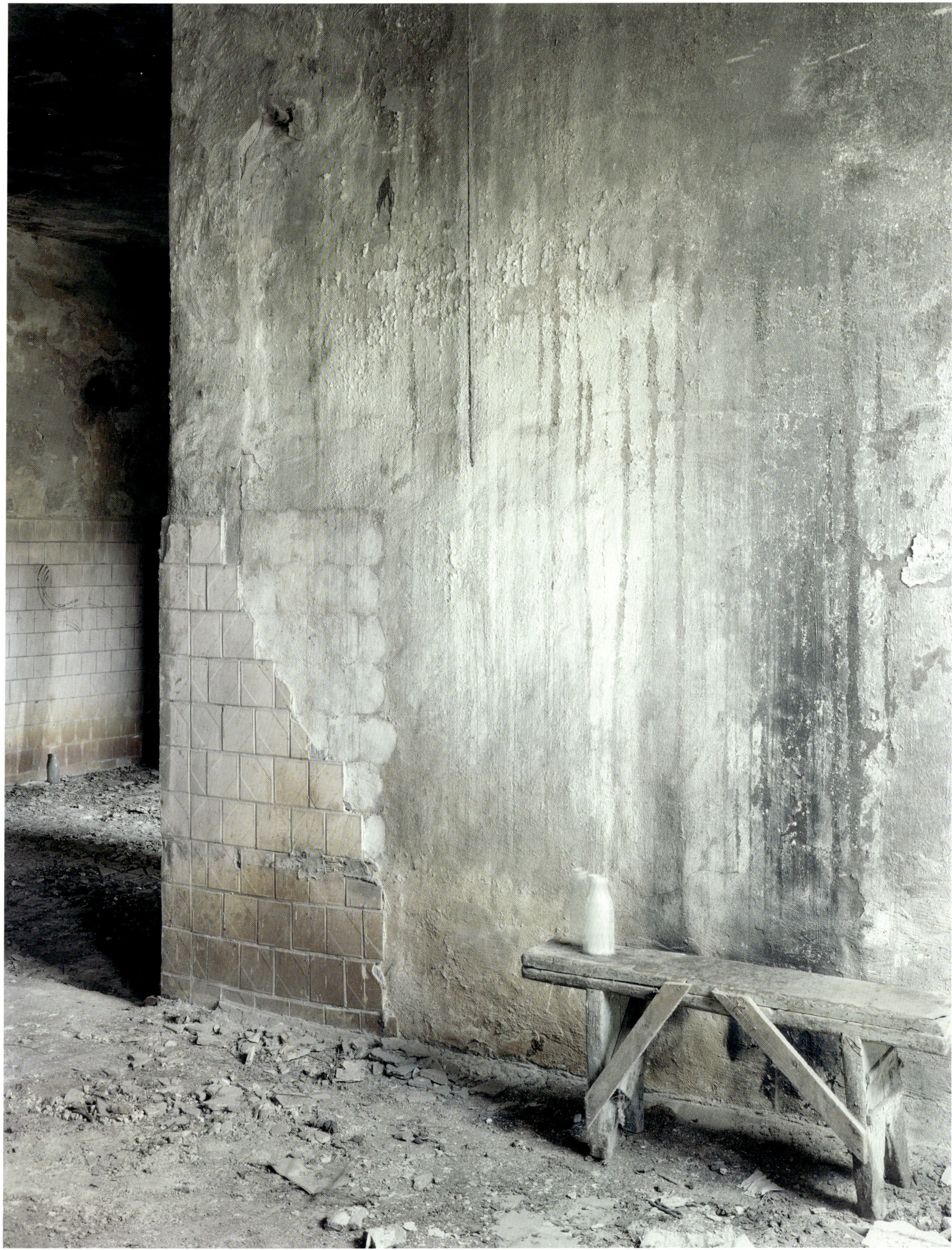

moloko II, 2012

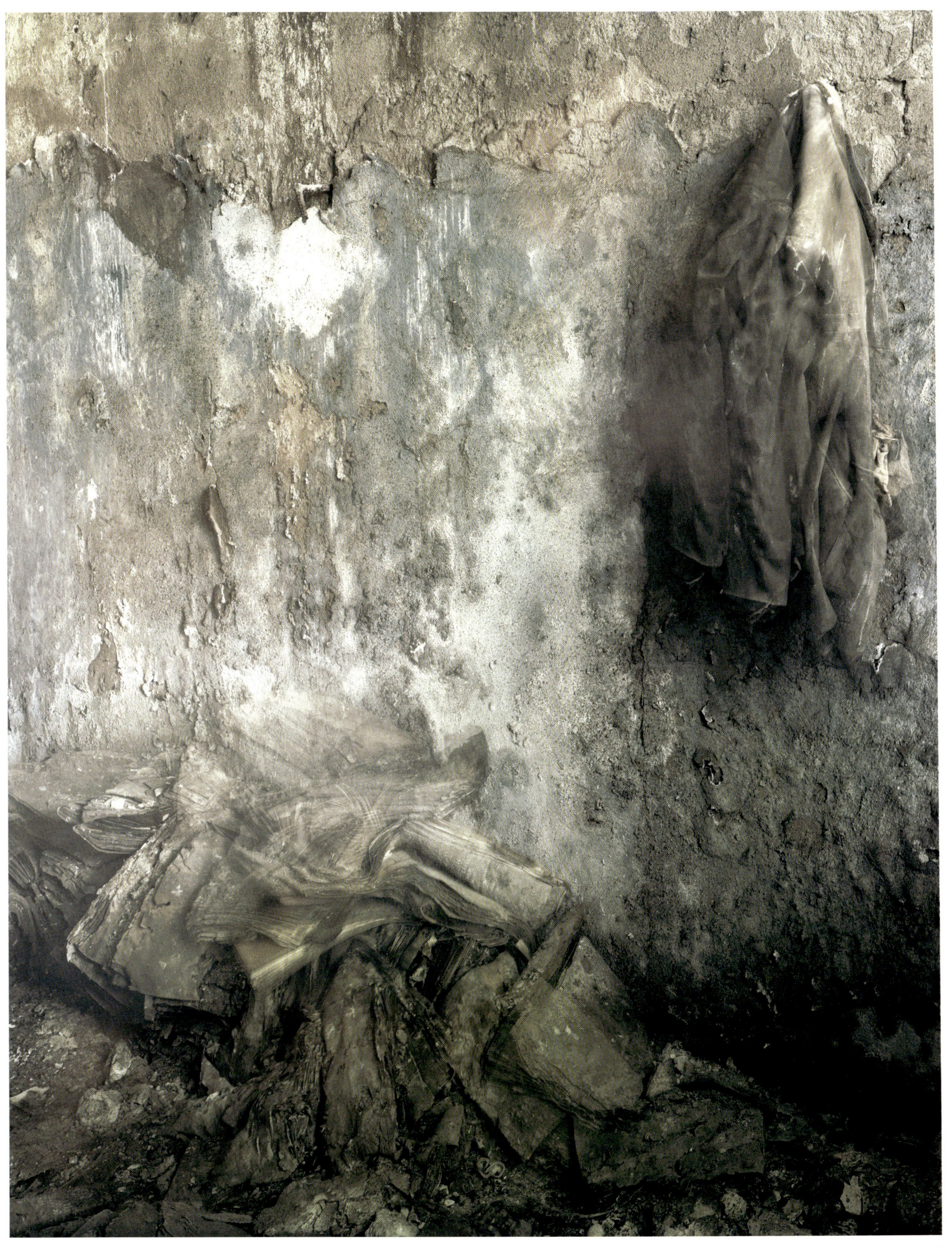

(Dé)composition, 2018

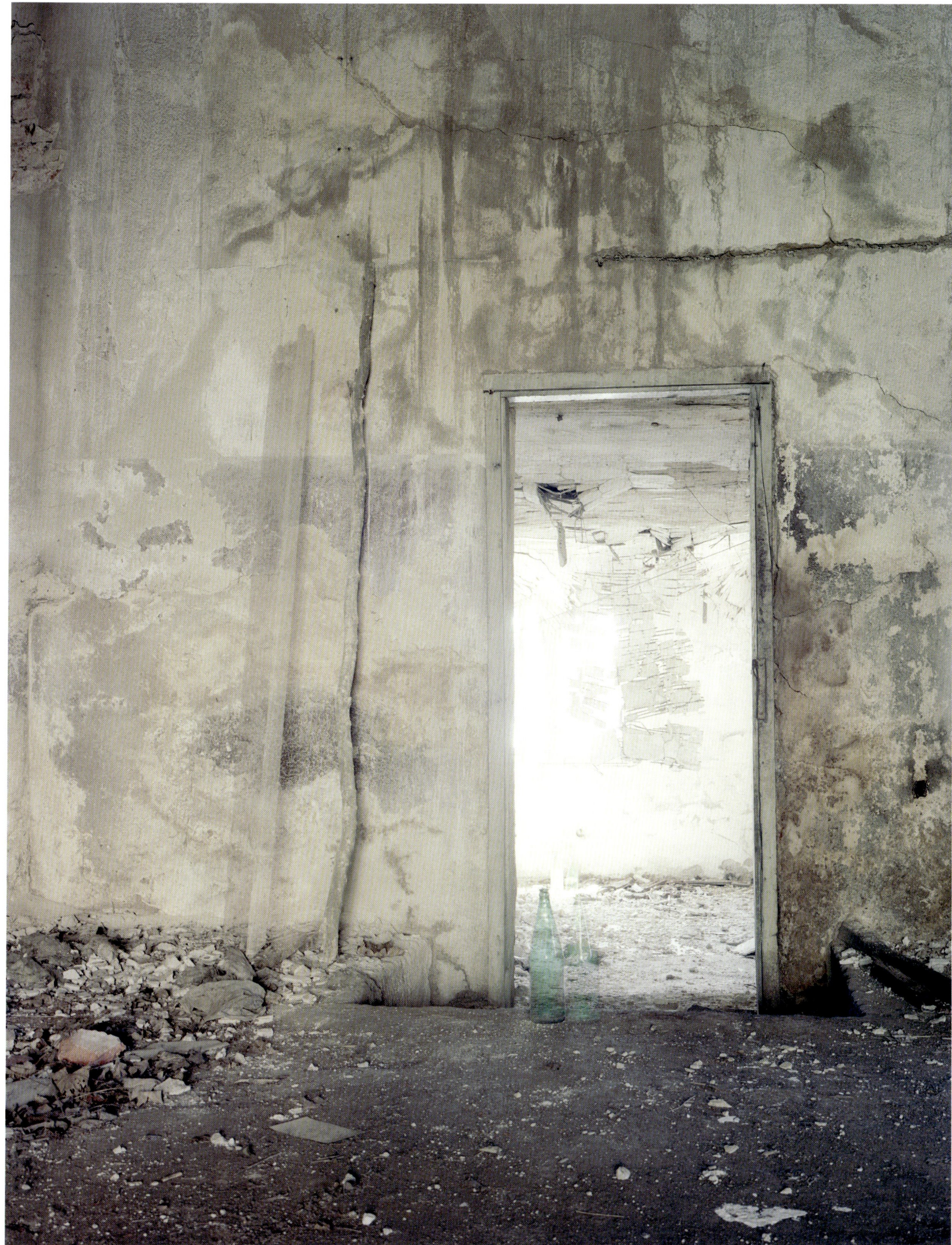

Pb-Schleier, 2015

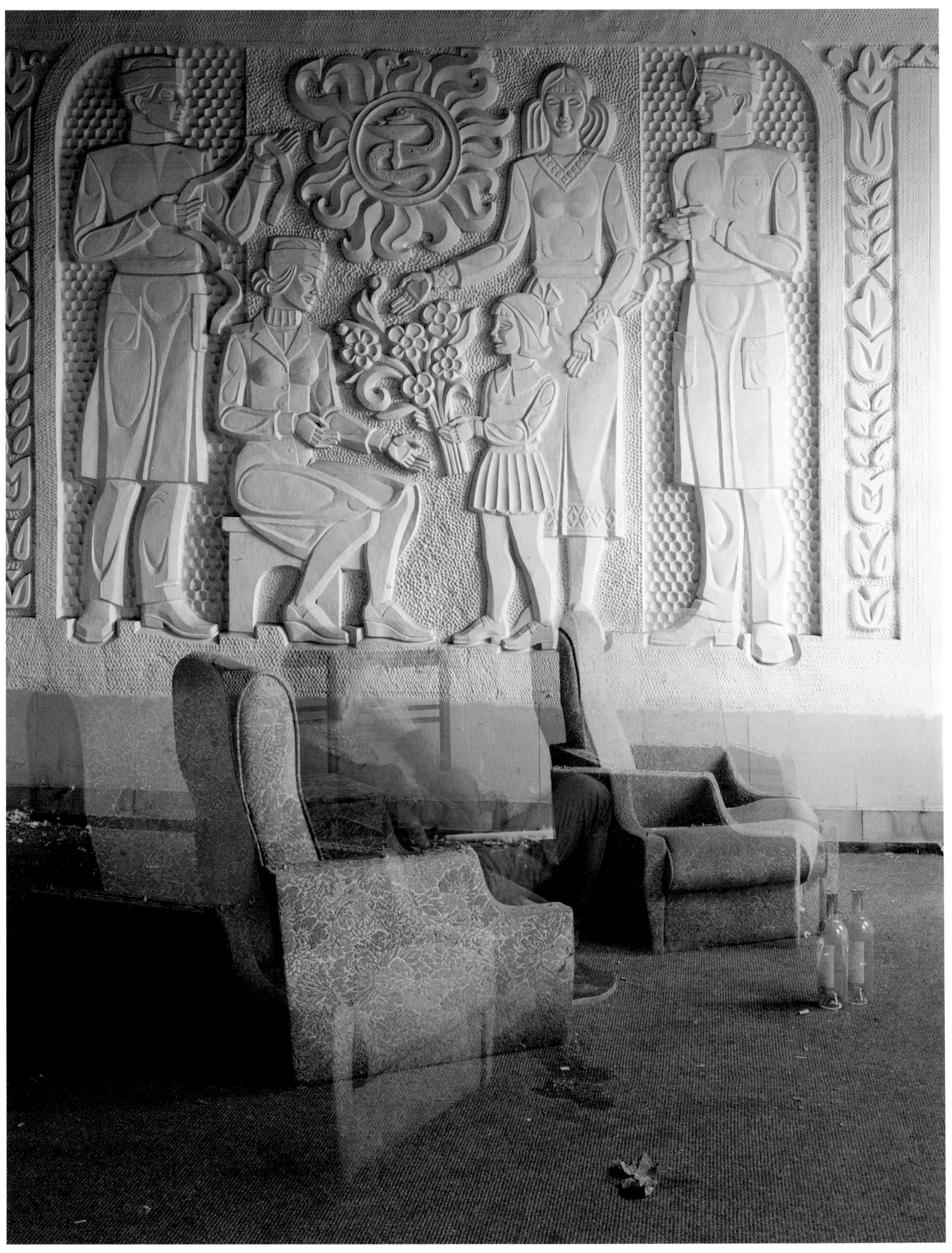

...im falschen Film, 2019

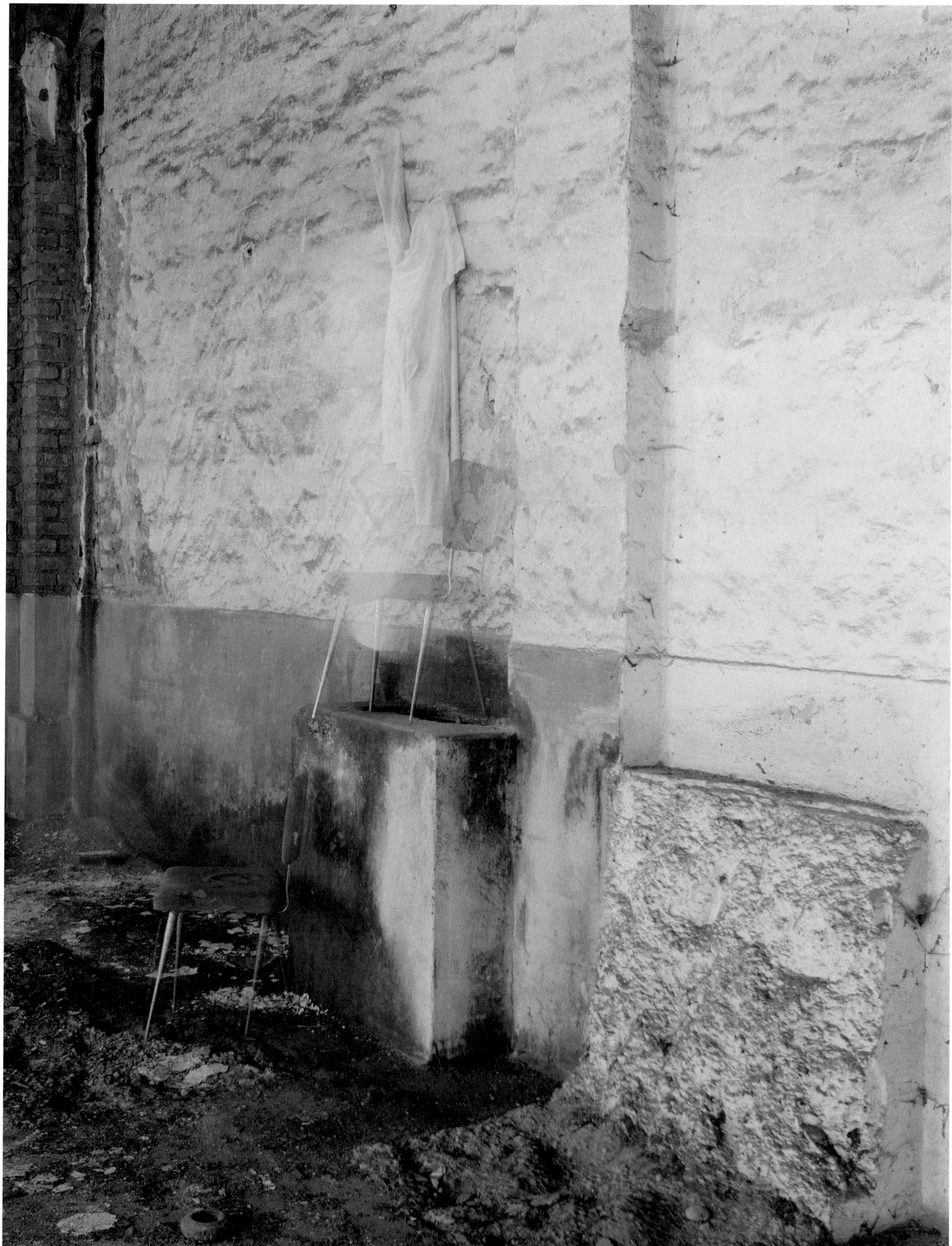

Monumentbesteigung, 2017

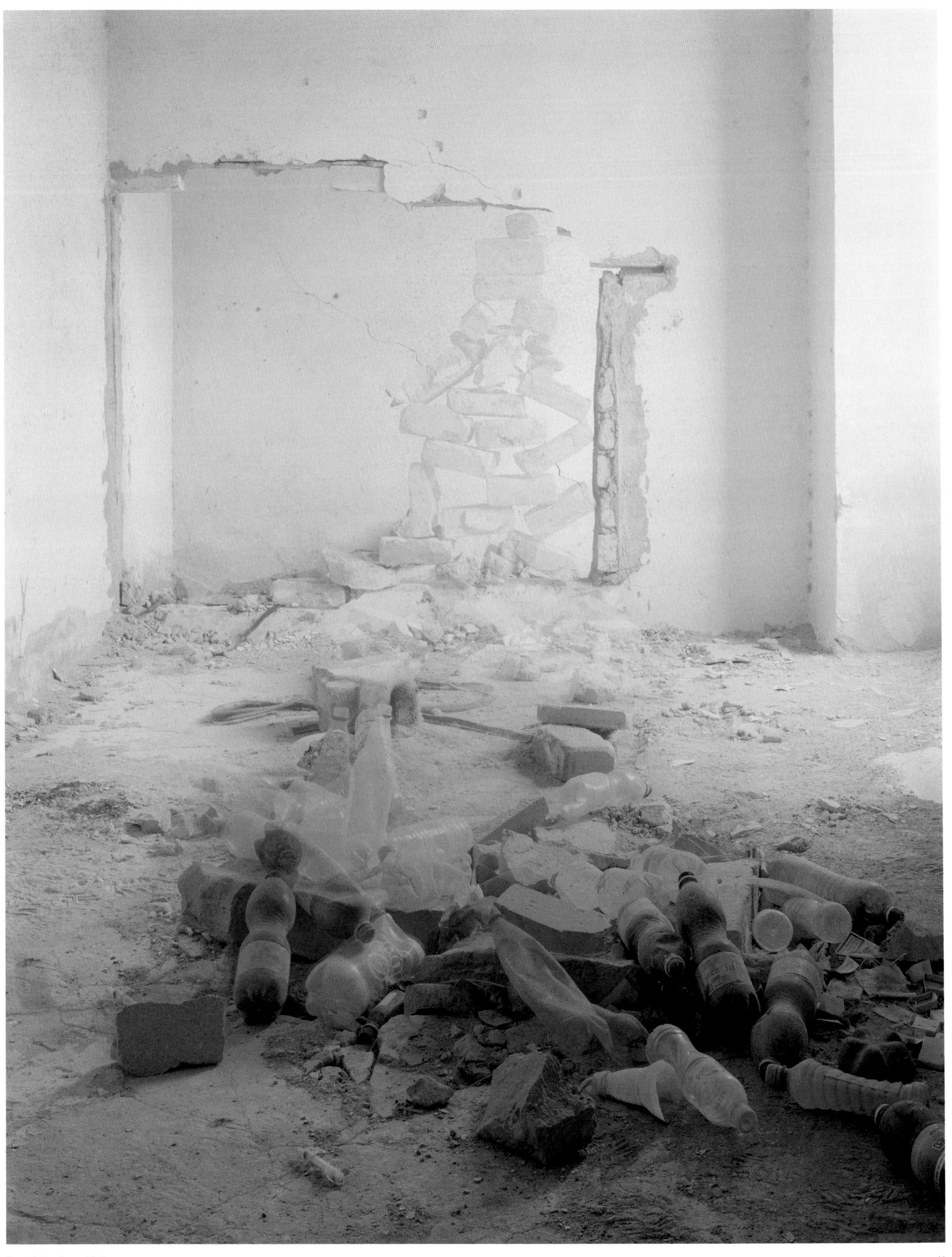

Der seichte Turm, 2018

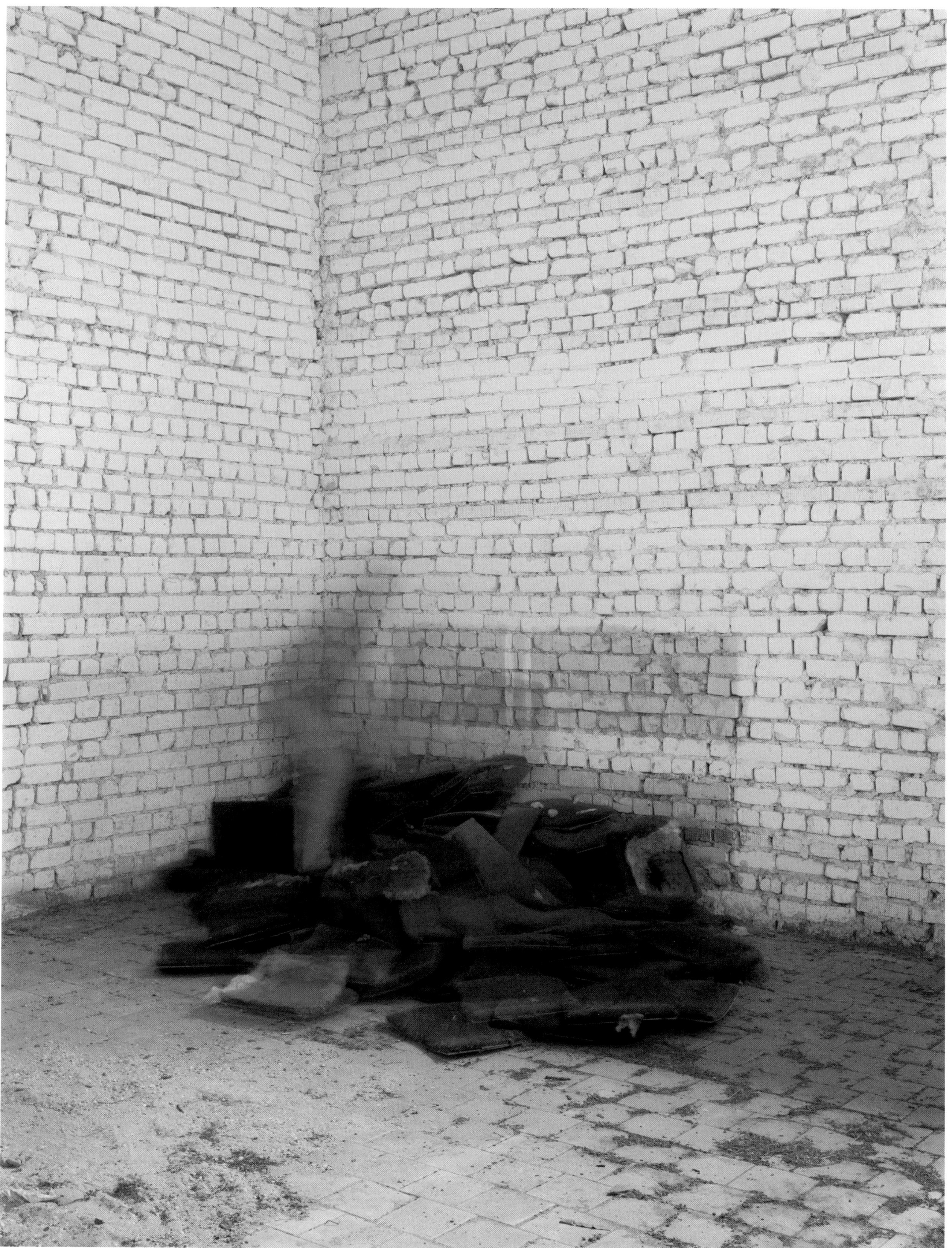

entropy, 2017

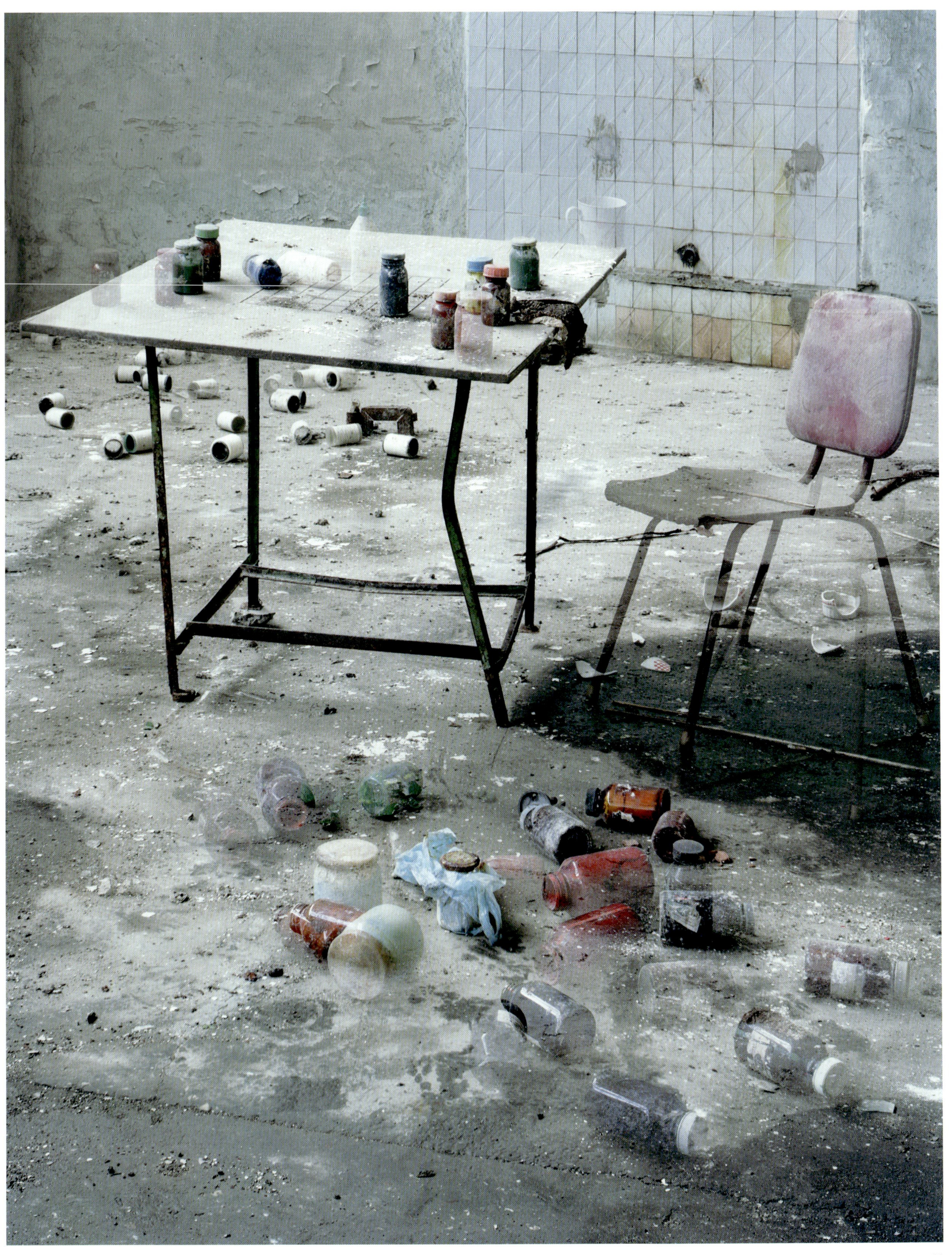

chess table, 2017 (detail)

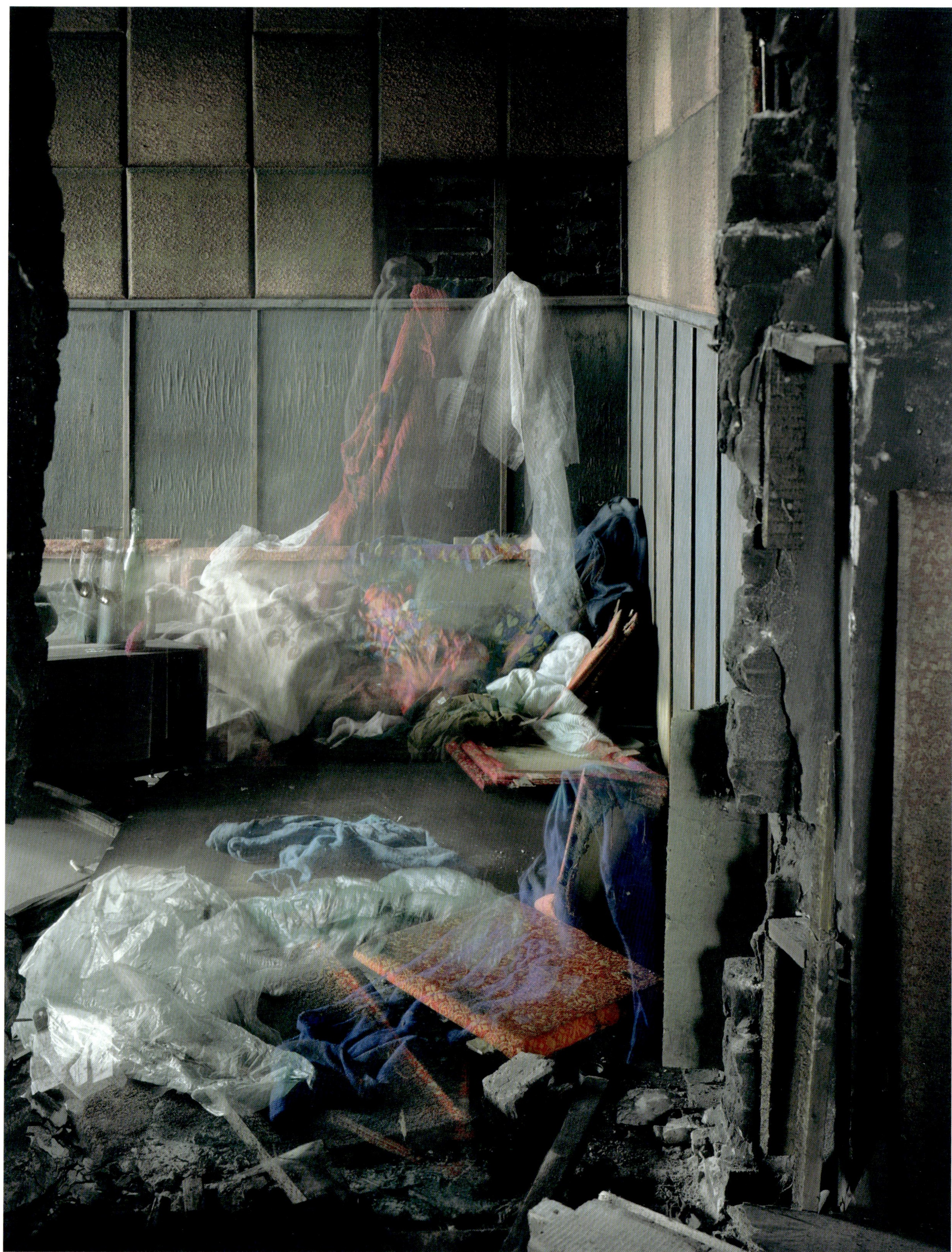

Des Kaisers neue Kleider, 2019

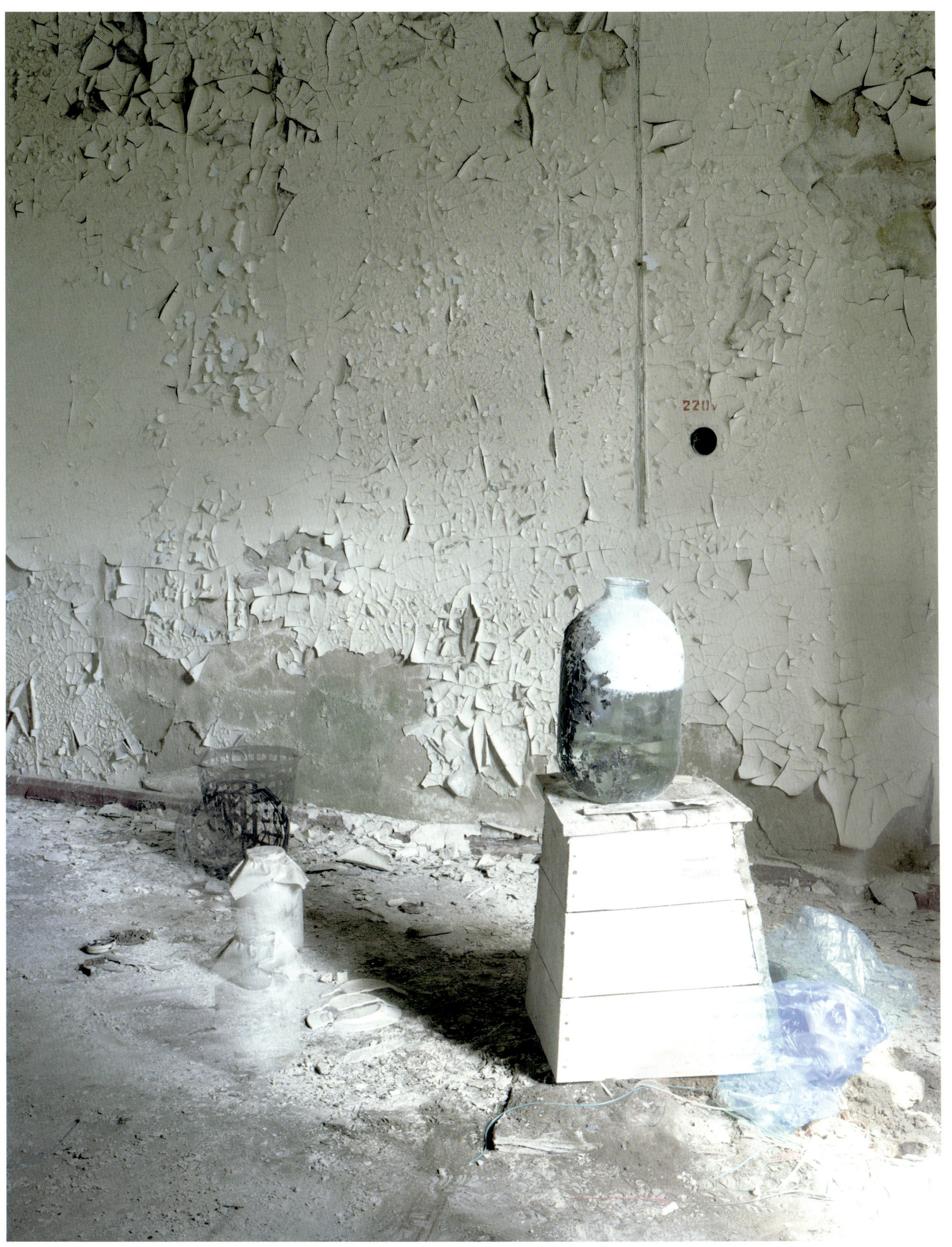

220V, 2018

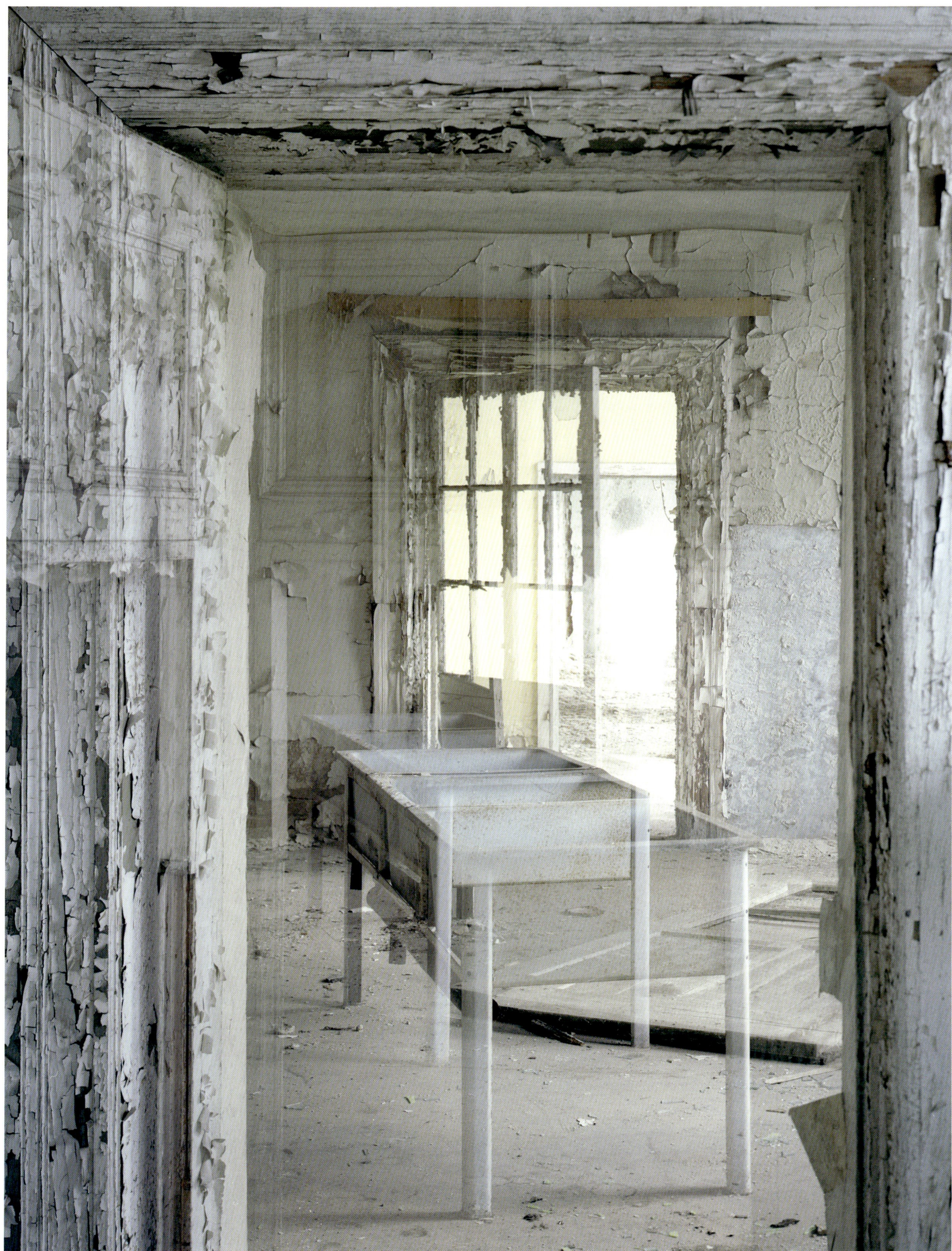

zwischen Tür & Angel, 2017

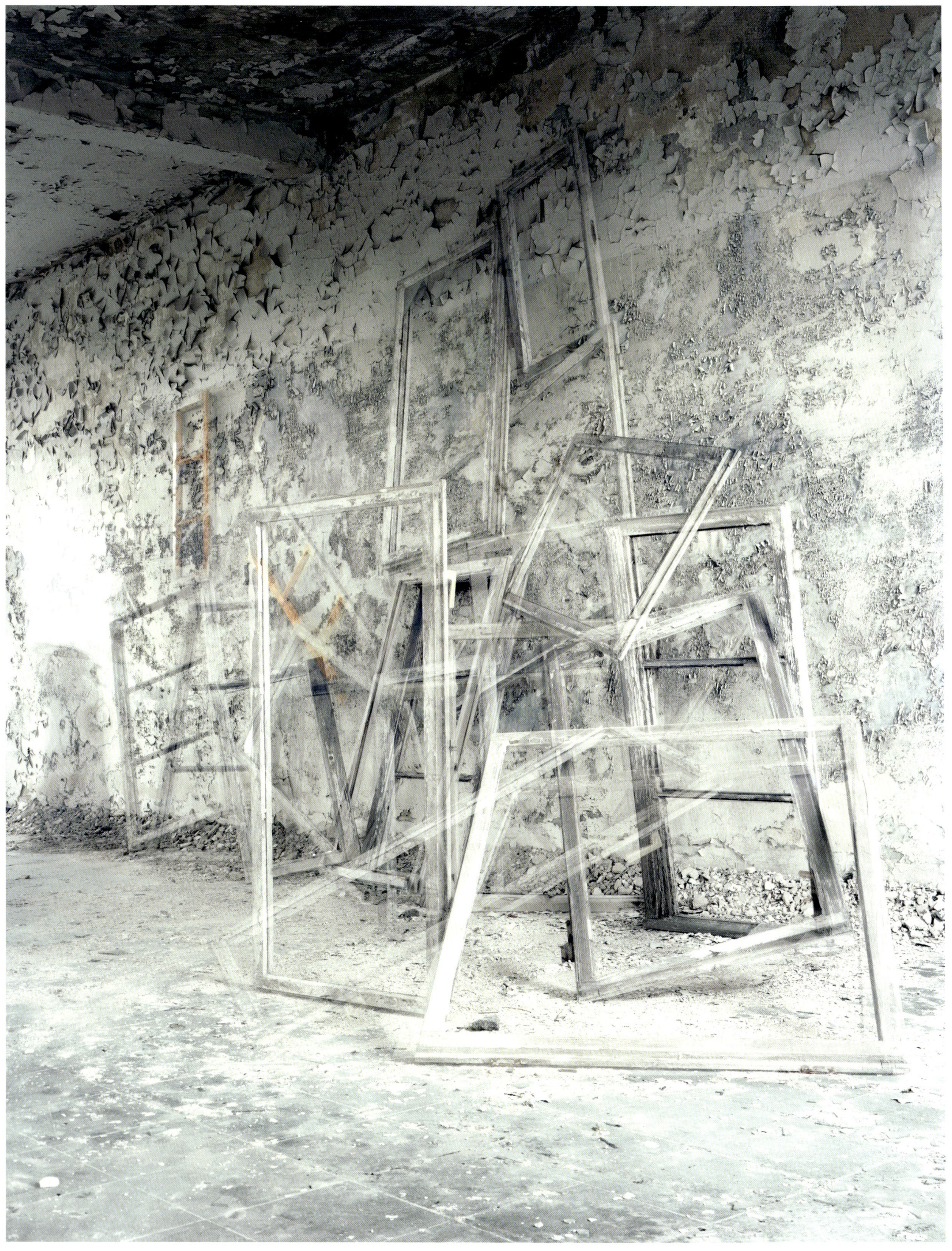

Babel tower I, 2018

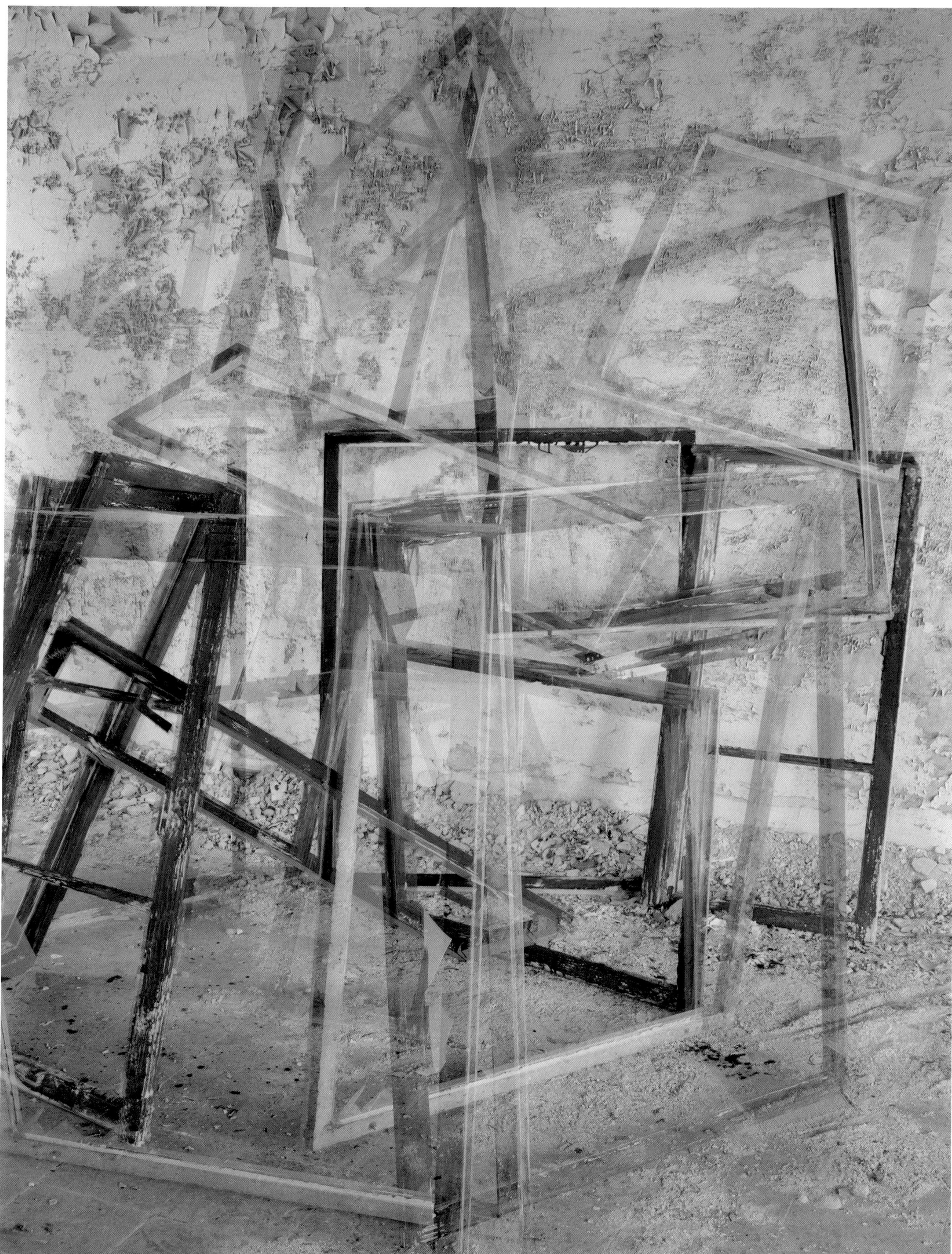

Babel tower III, 2018

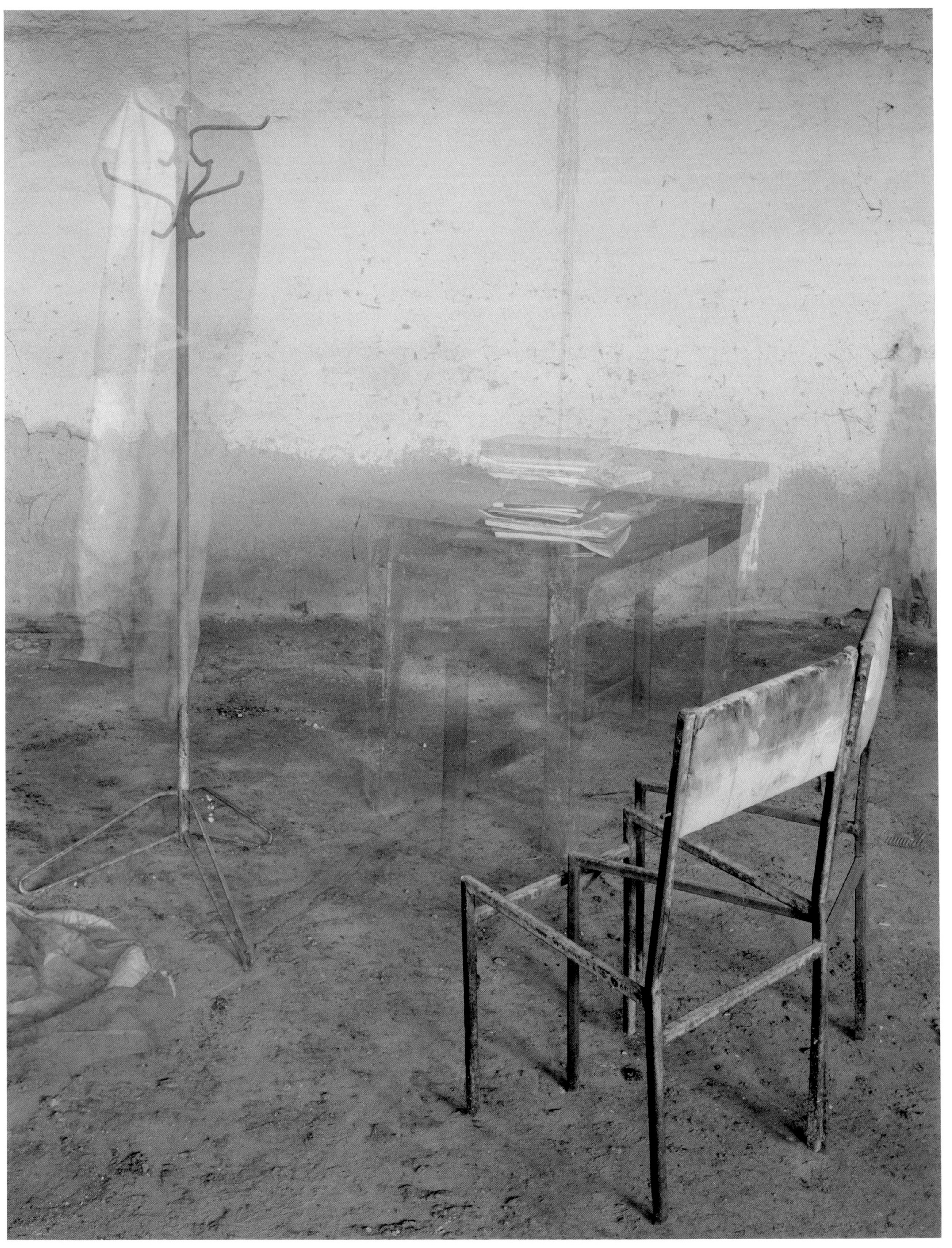

Tischtausch I, 2015

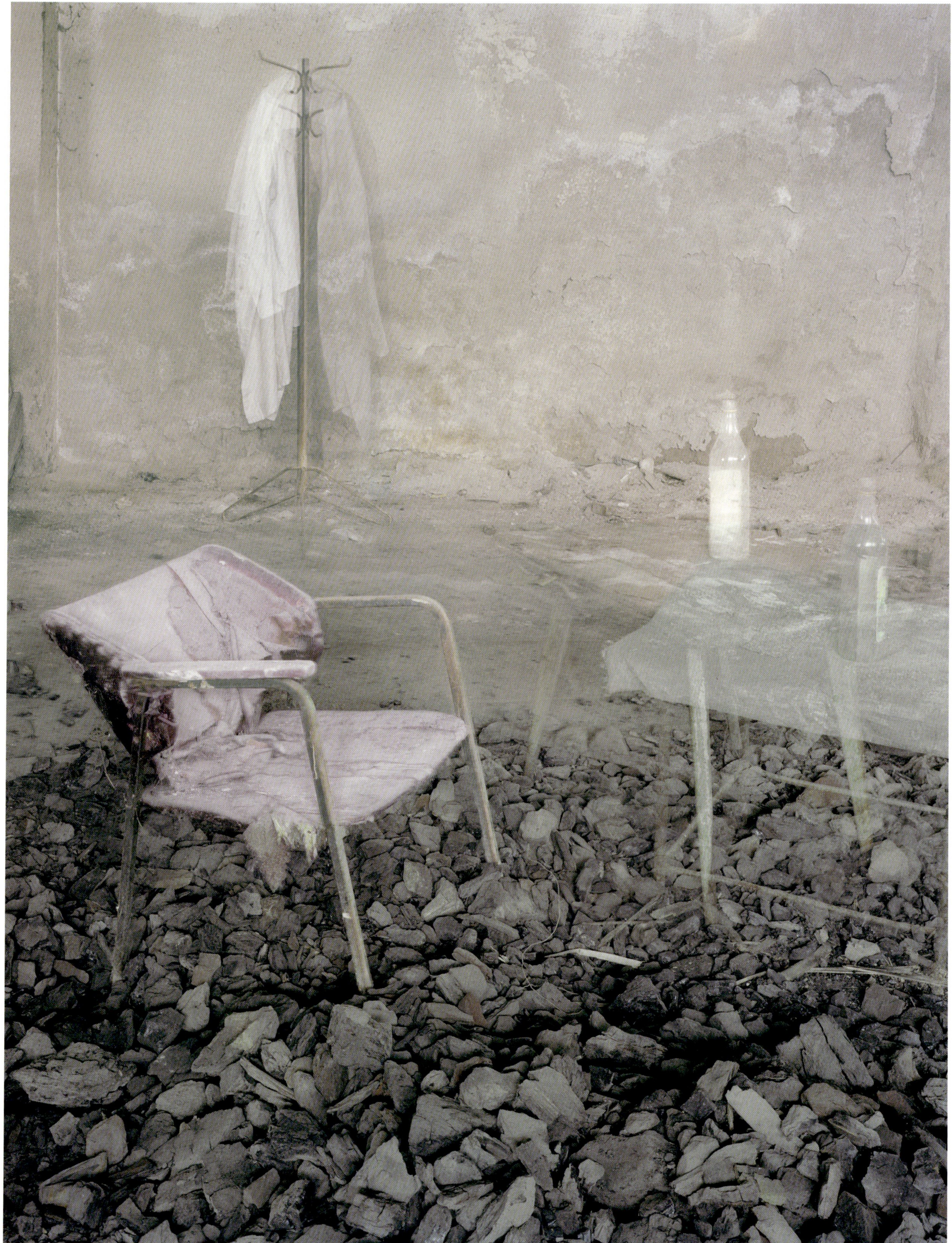

Tischtausch II, 2015

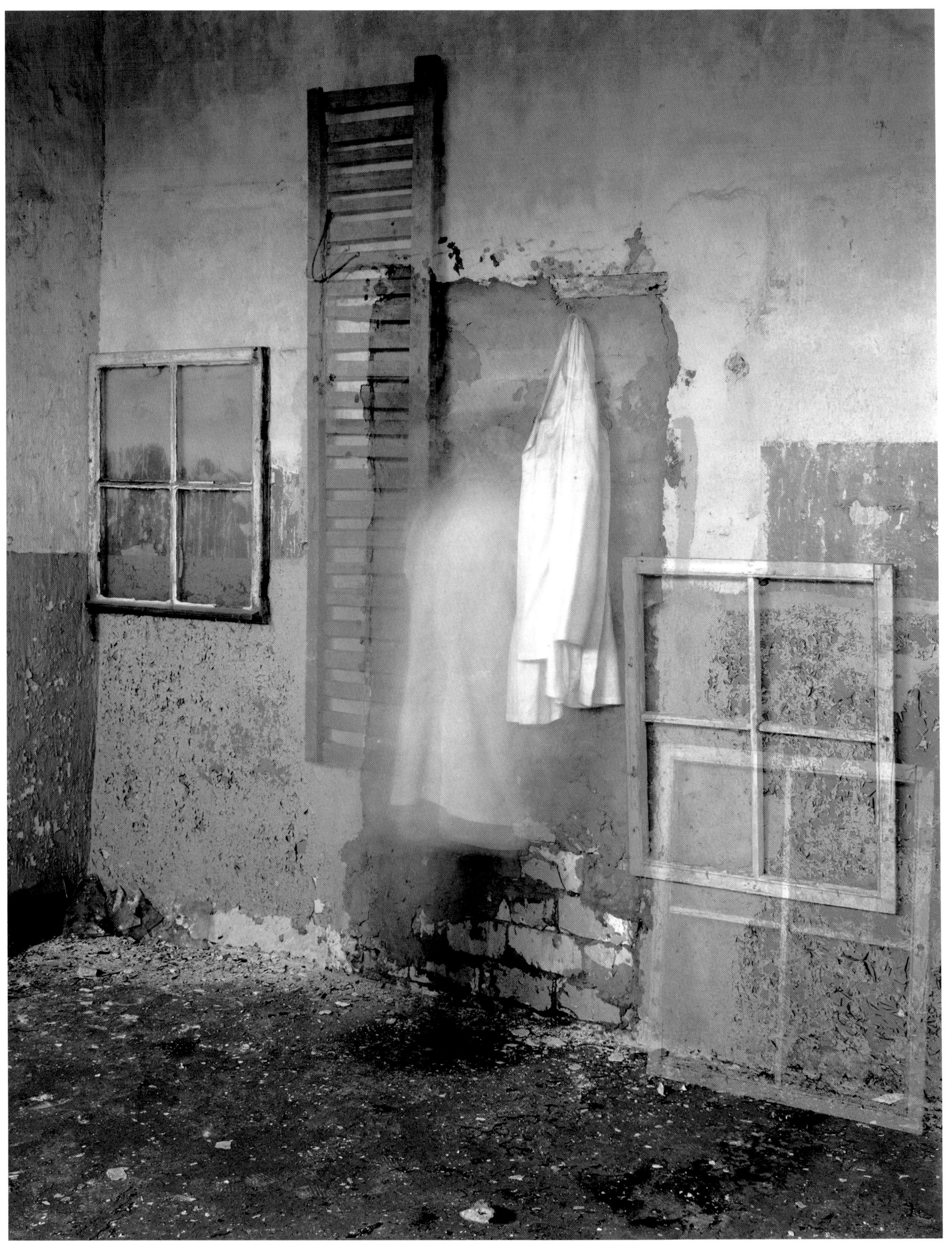

Der Prozeß, 2014

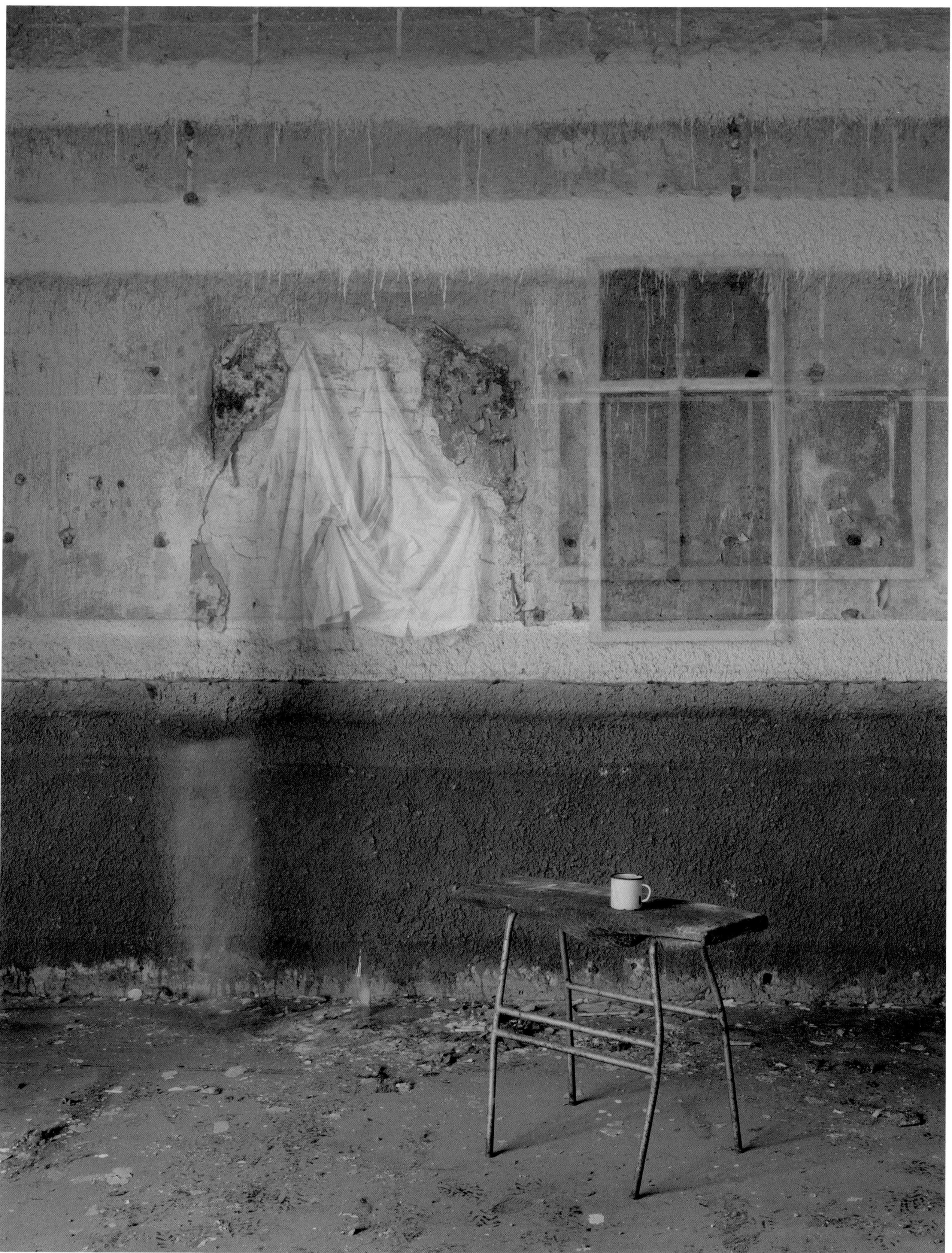

Thronflüchtiger, 2014

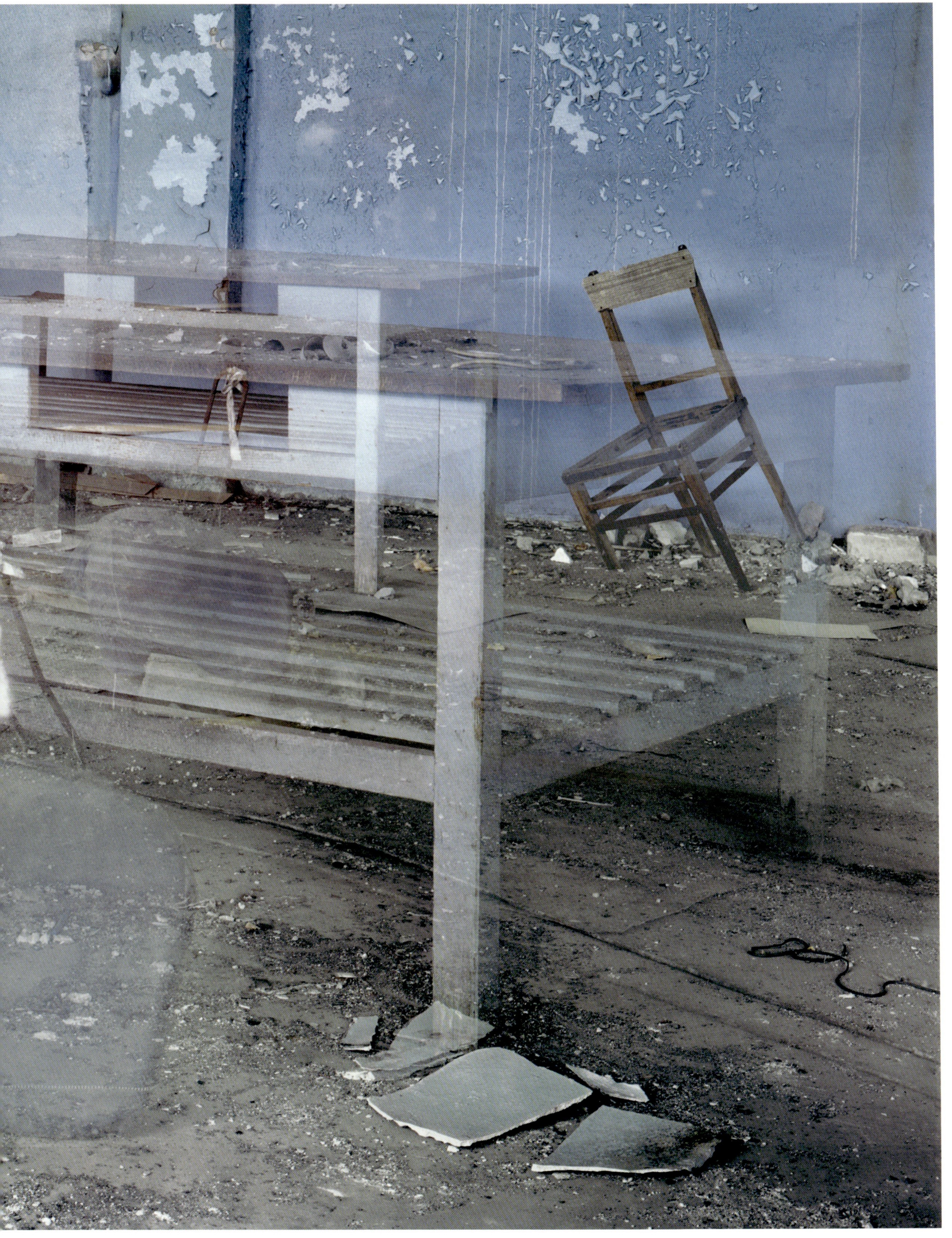

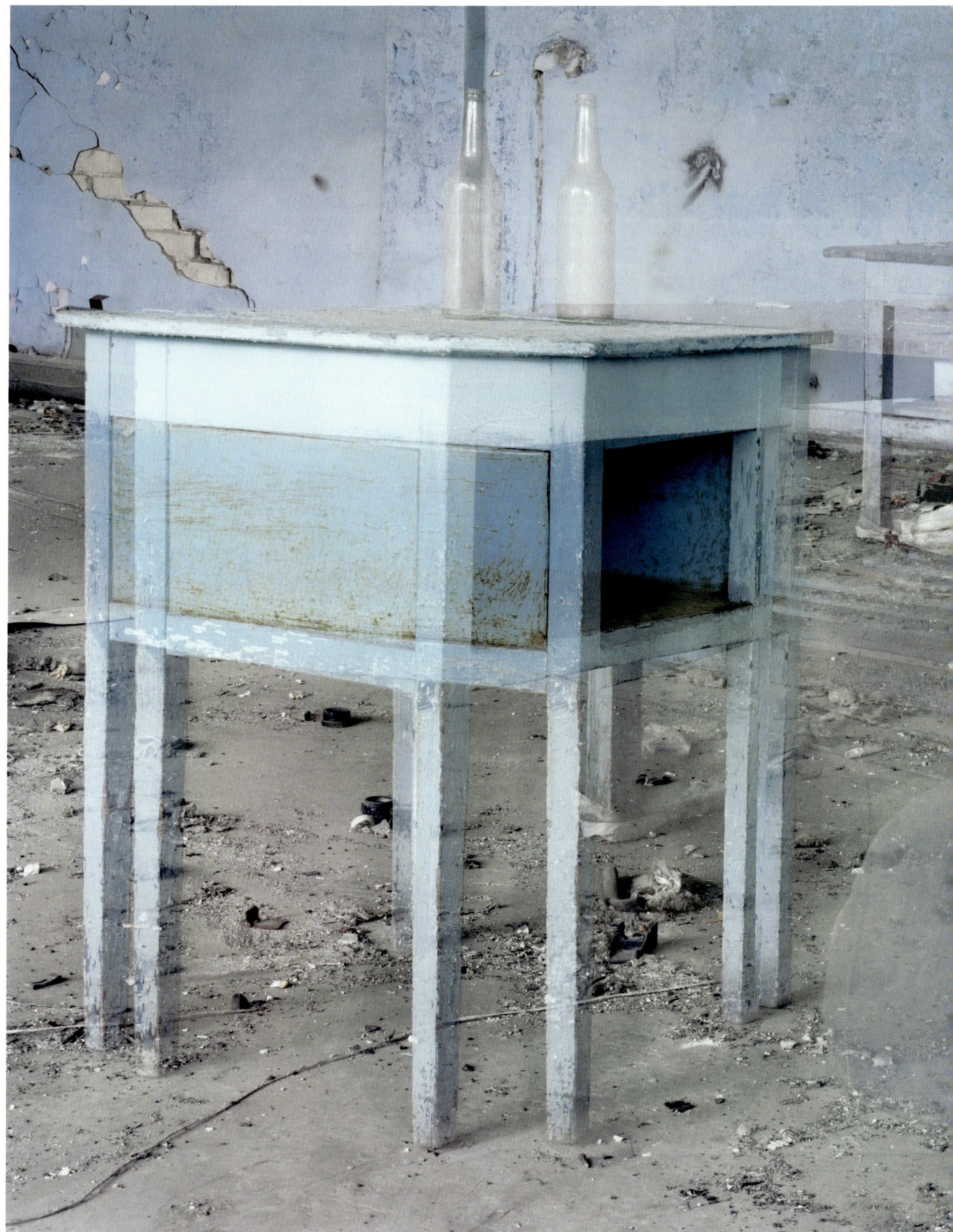

Kippstuhl, 2020 (detail)

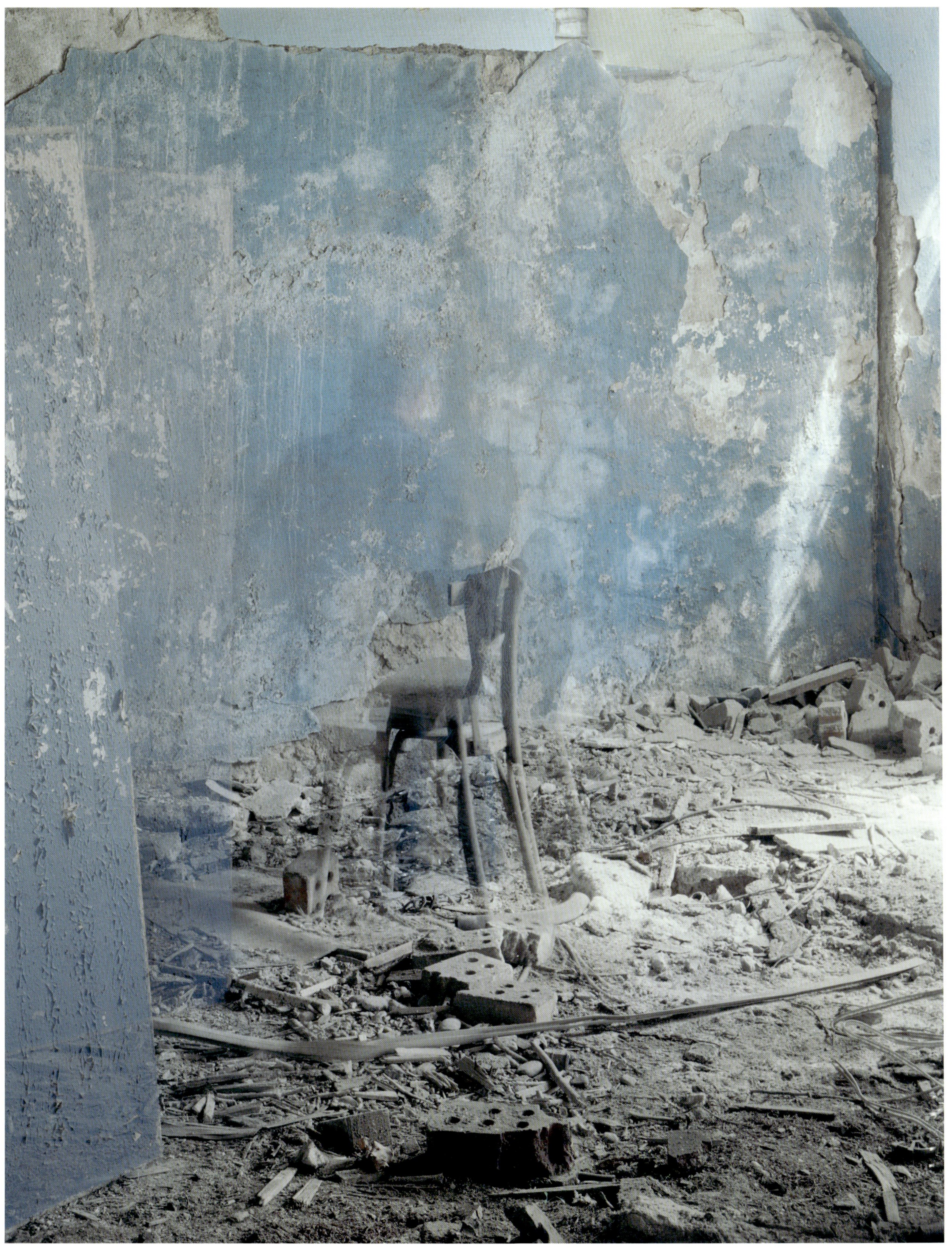

between blue walls, 2018

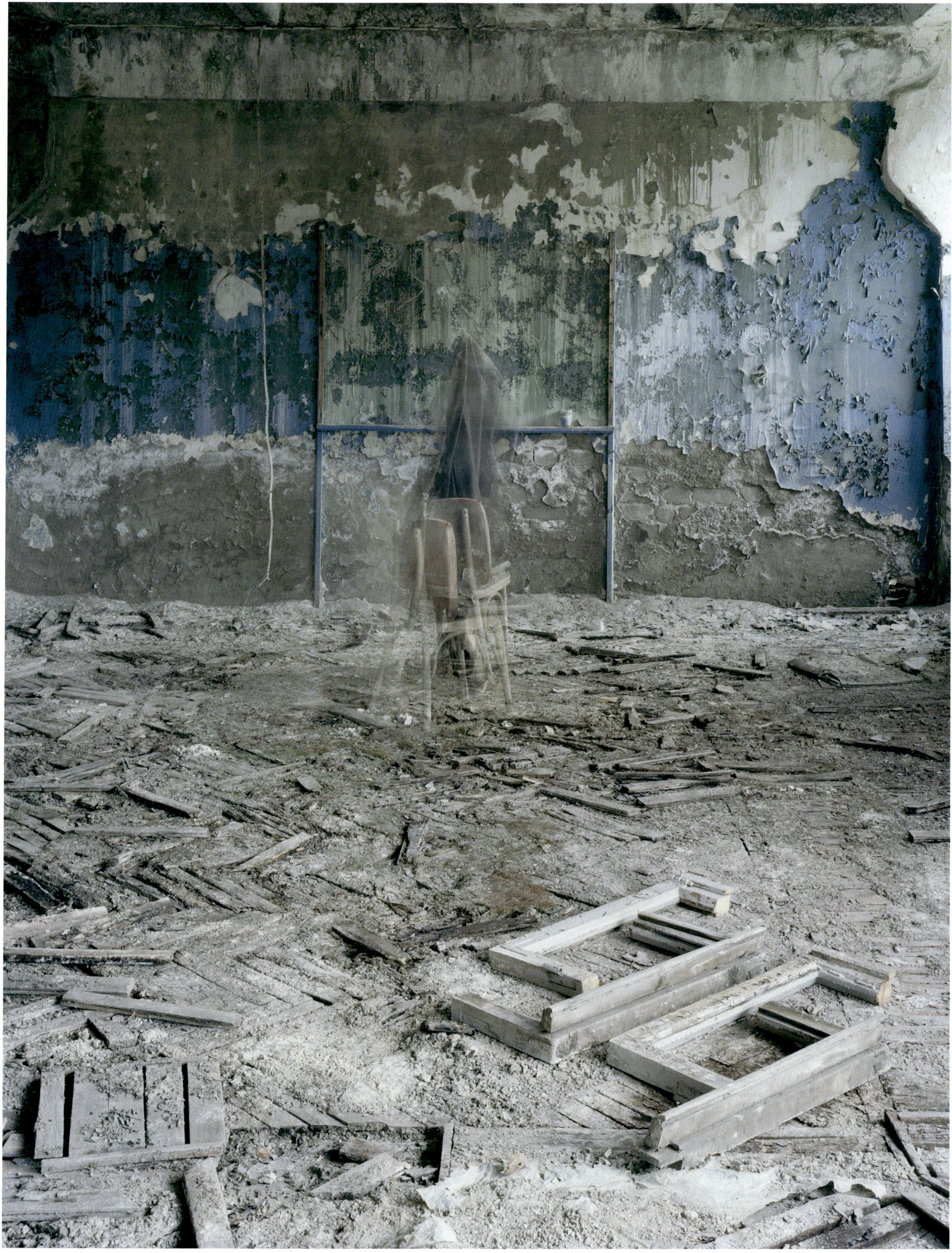

§§, 2018

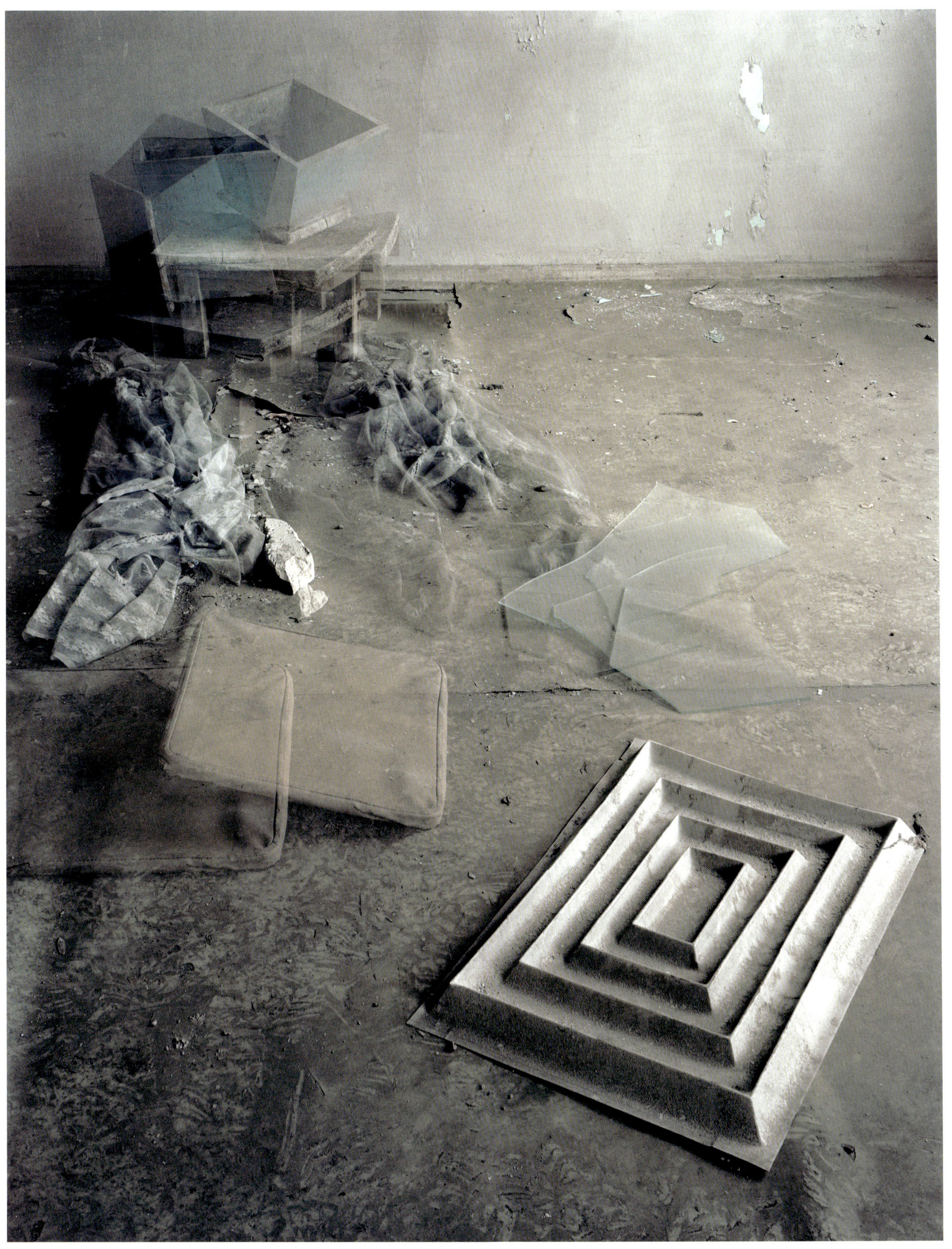

rhombus, quadrat & kegelstumpf, 2018

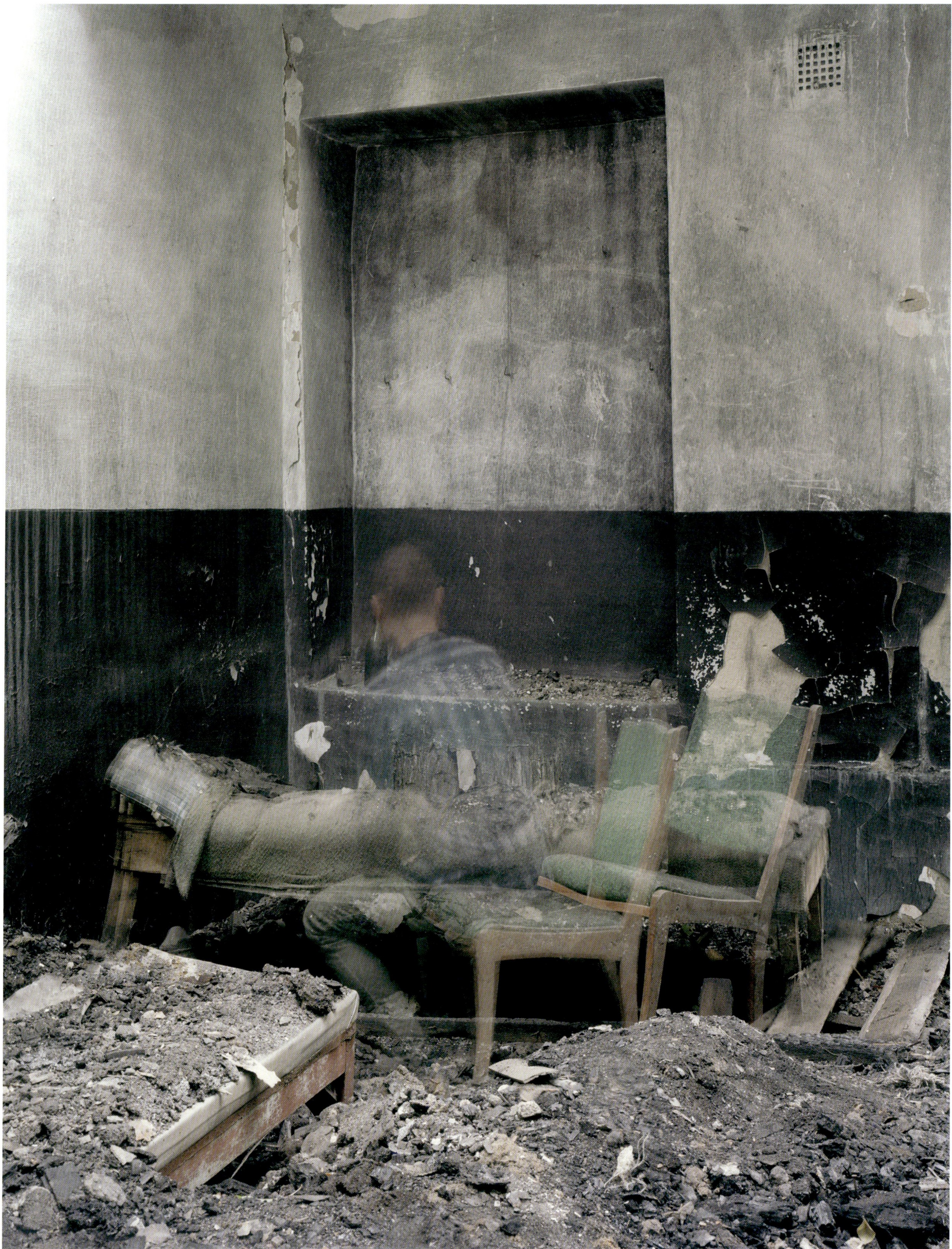

Pietà, 2019

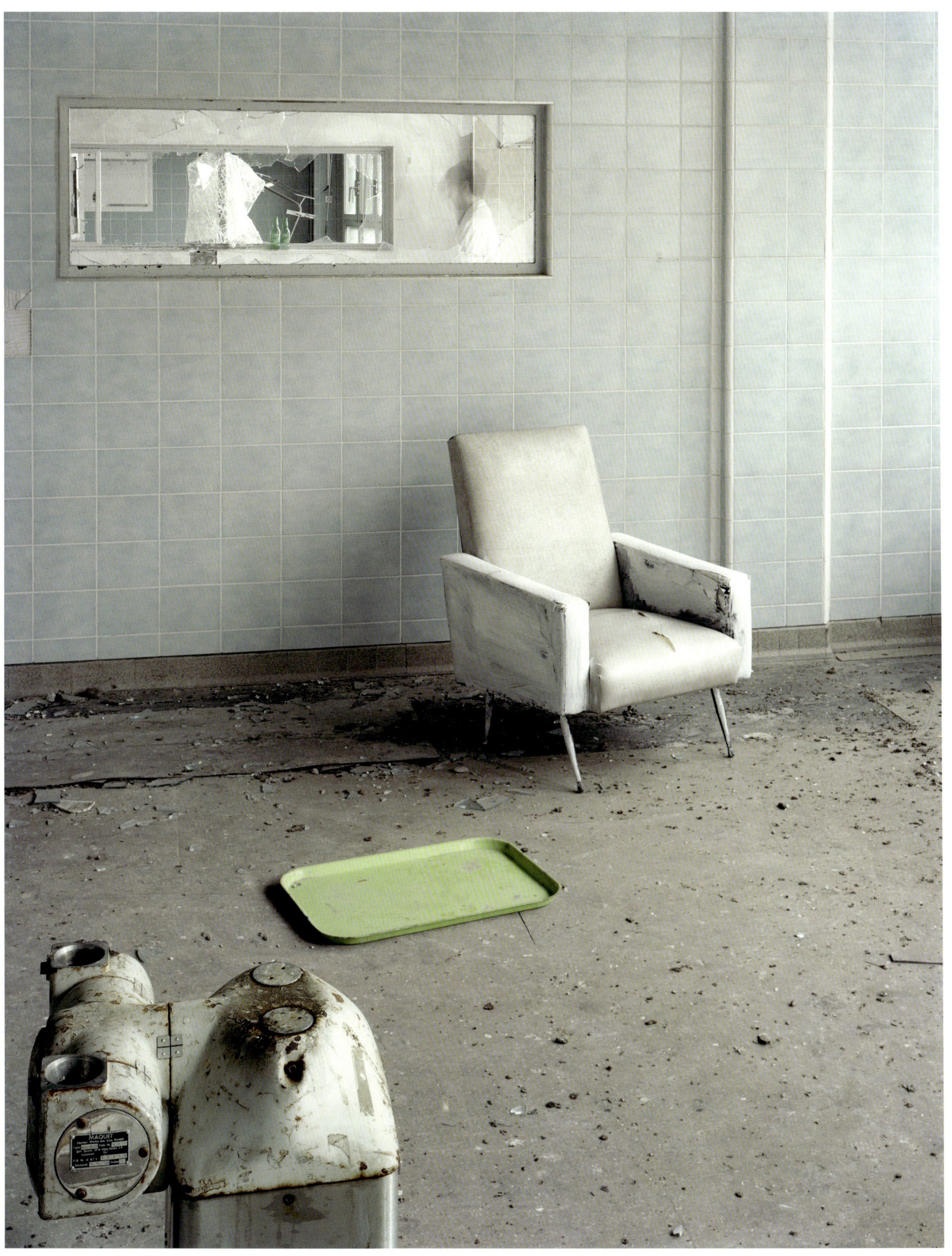

my favorite pet, 2015

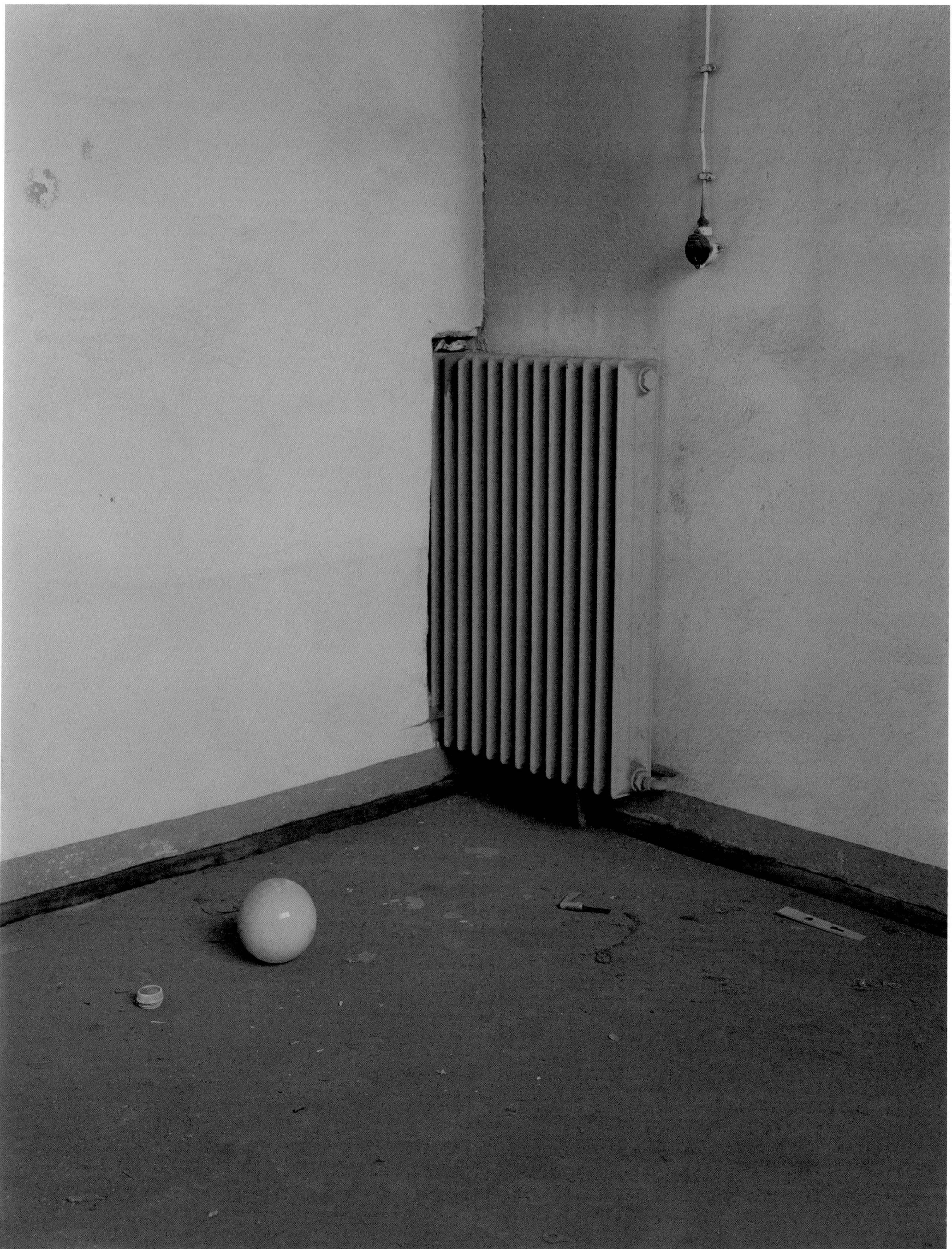

Das Verhör, 2020

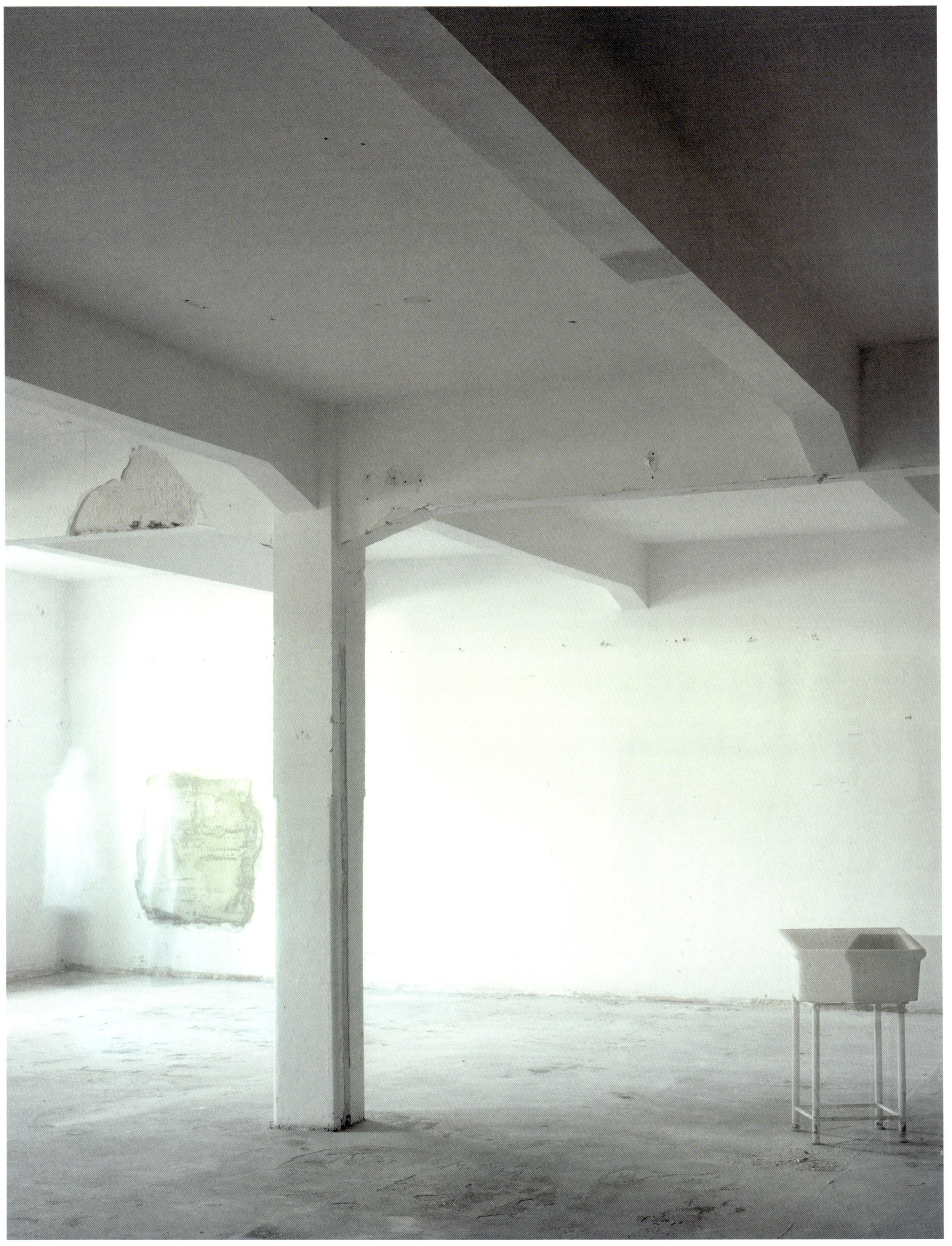

Zwielichtiger, 2013

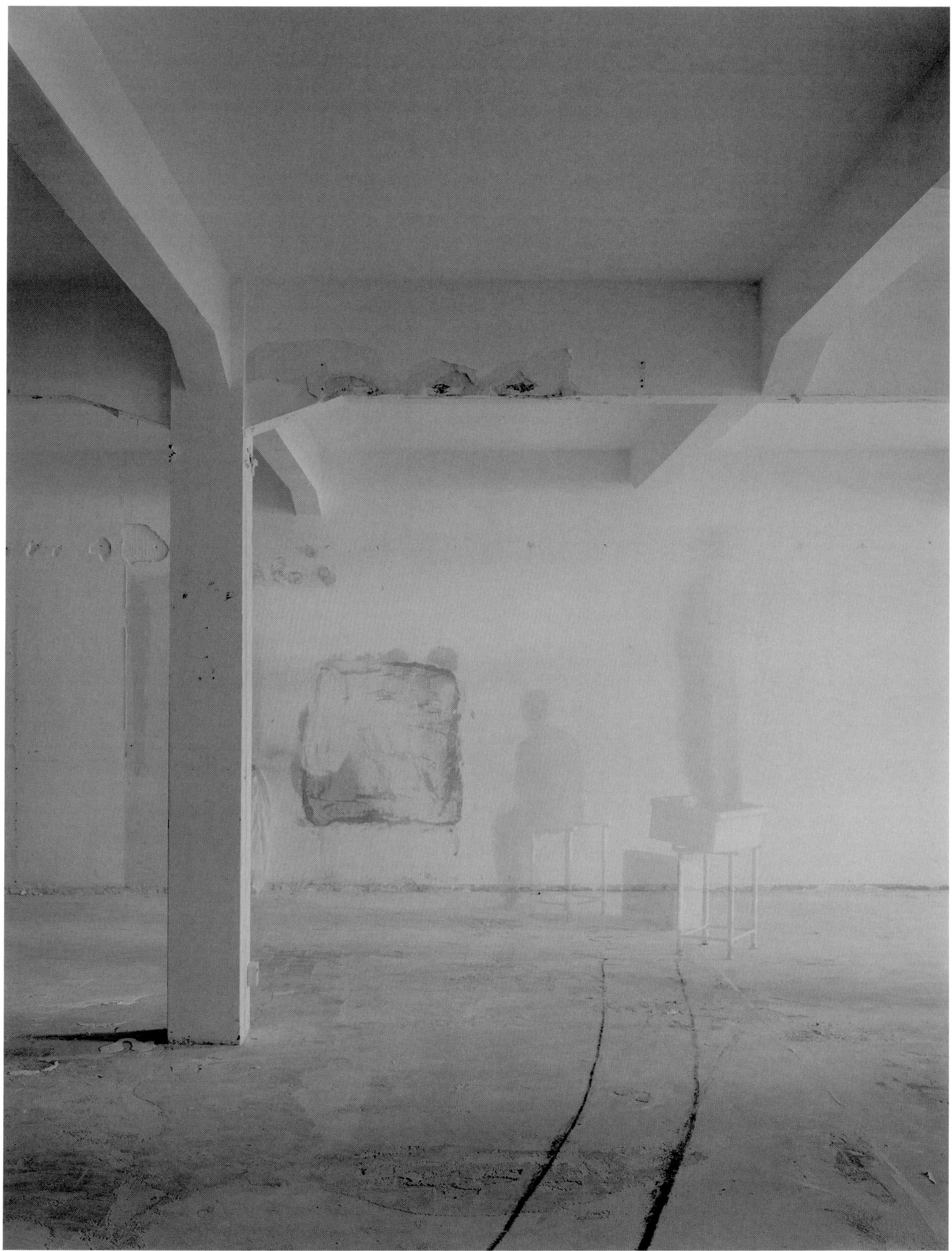

schau-Spiel, 2013

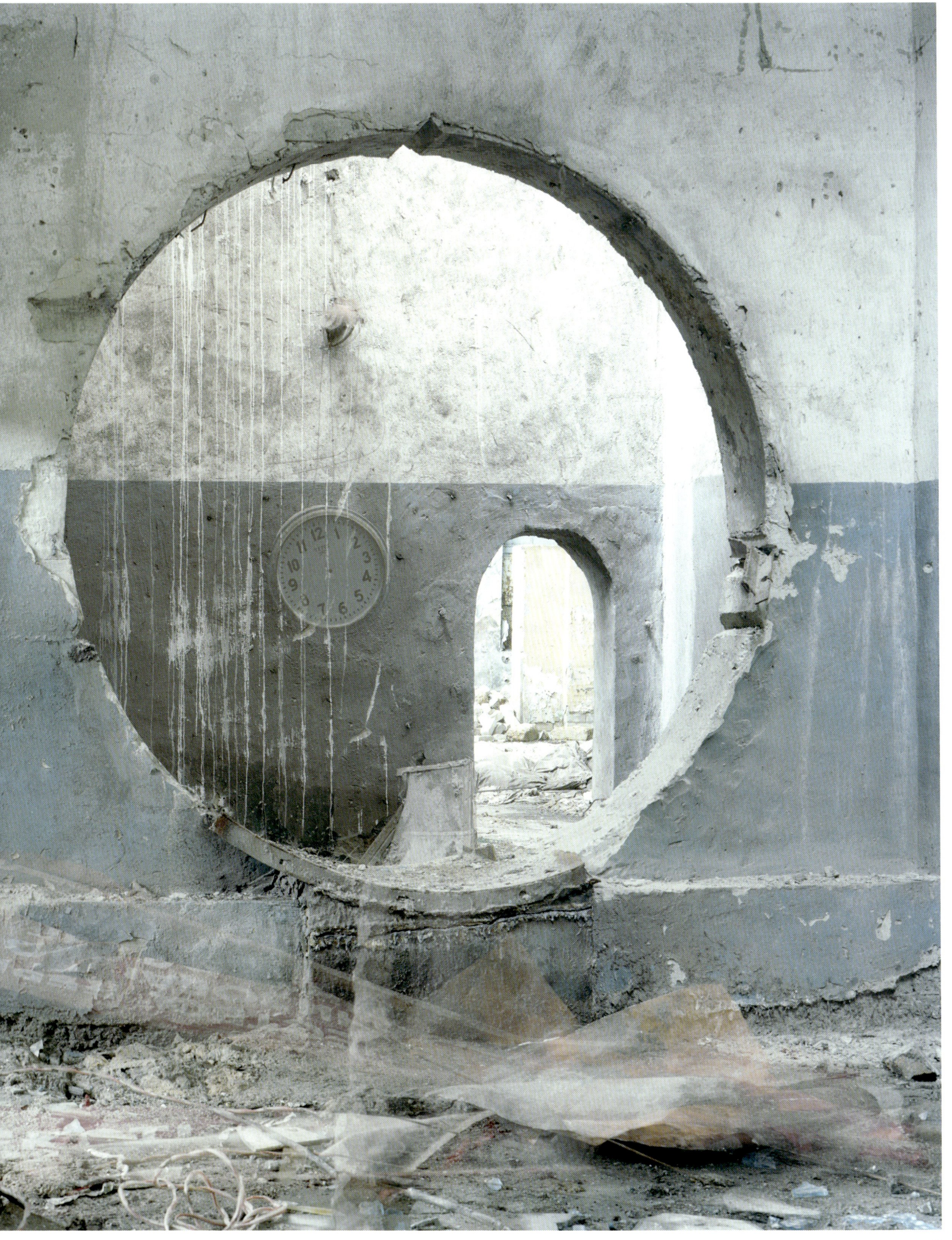

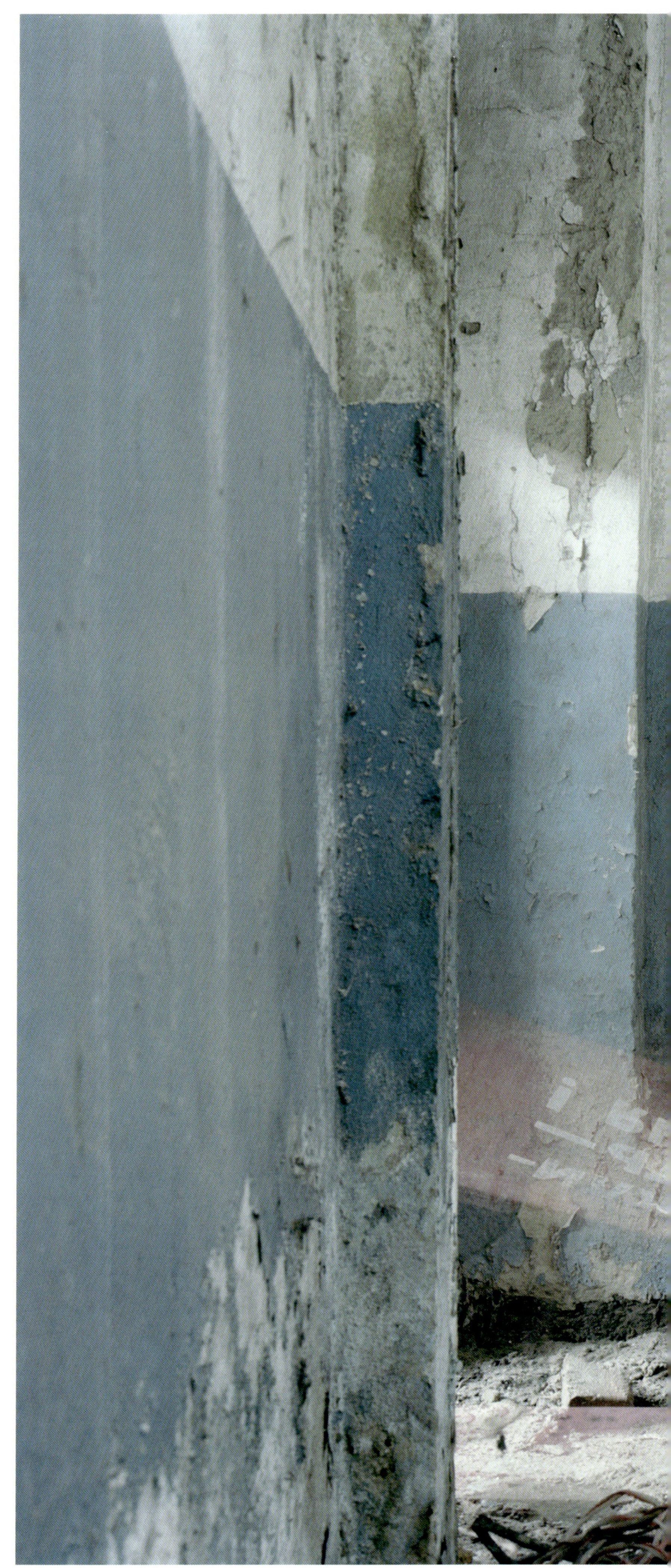

Zeigerlosigkeit, 2017

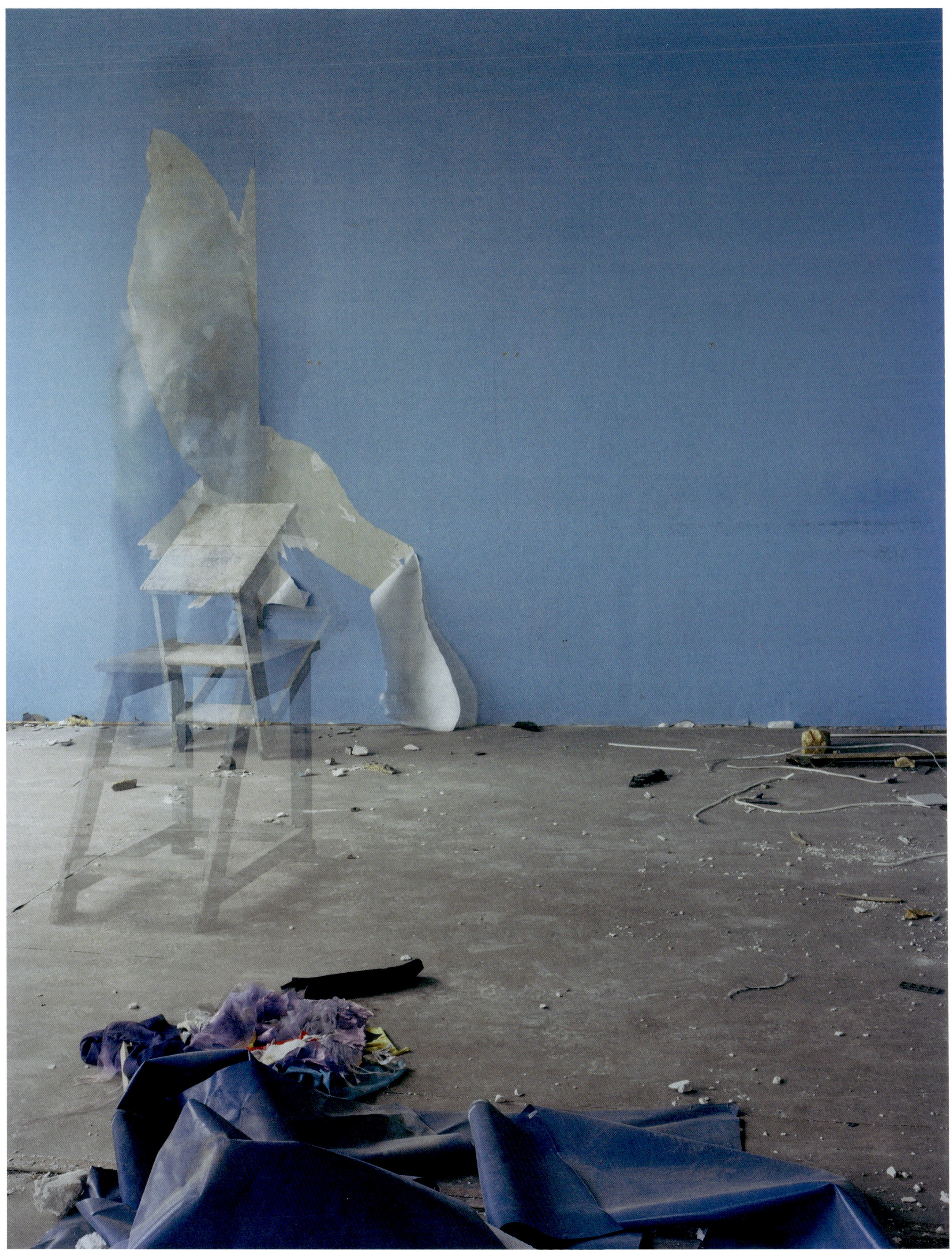

sky scraper, 2017

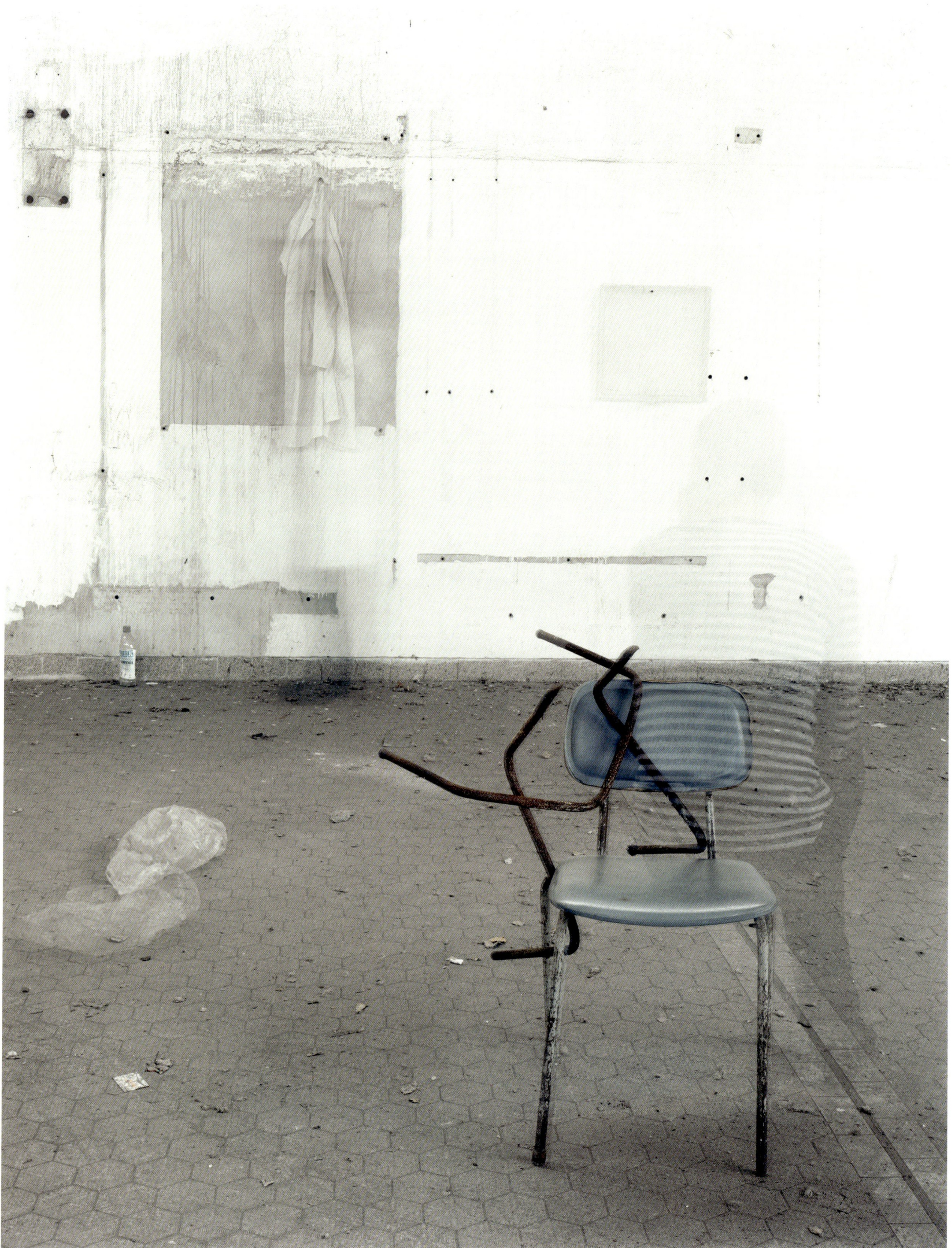

apiary, 2012

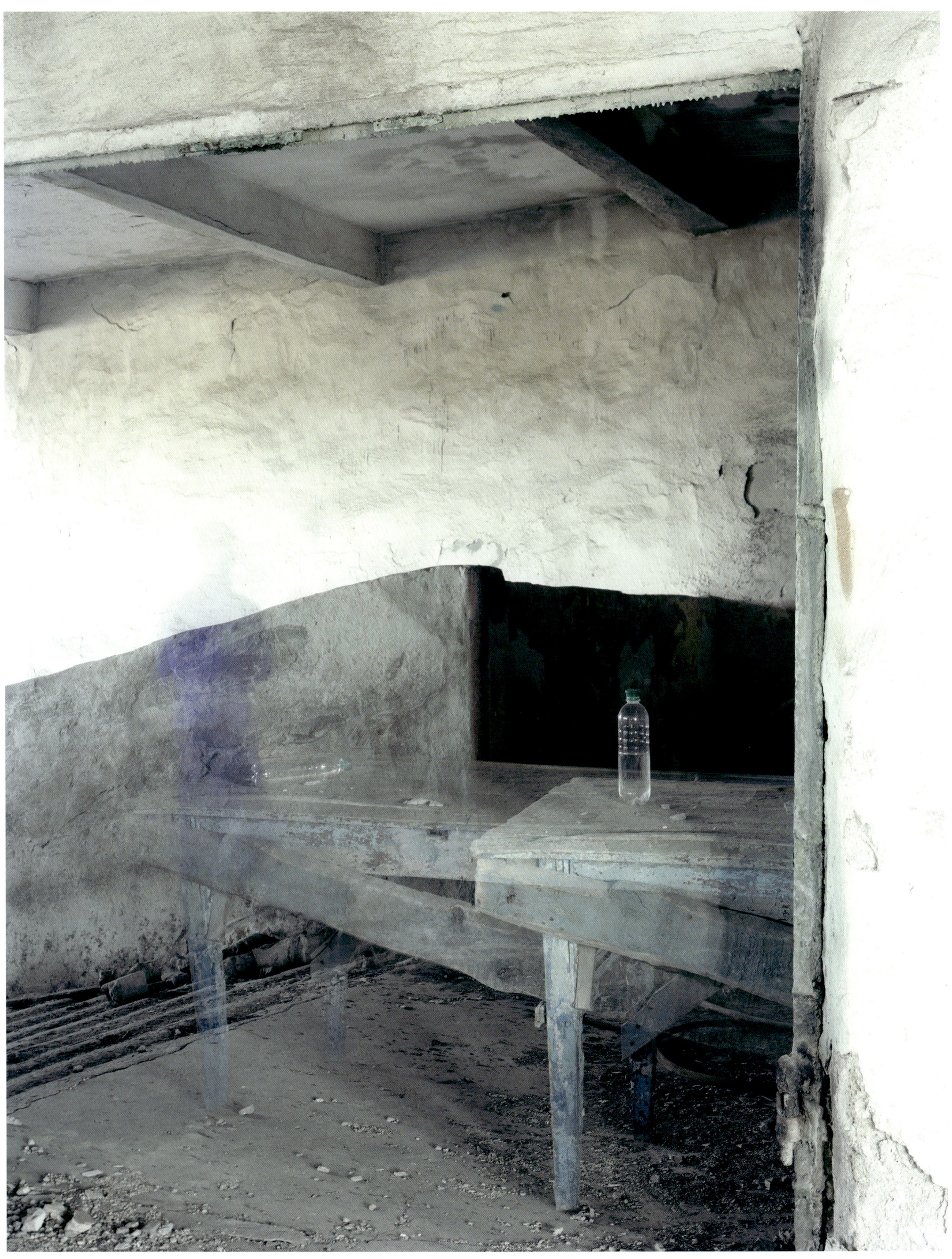

wandelndes Elixier, 2012

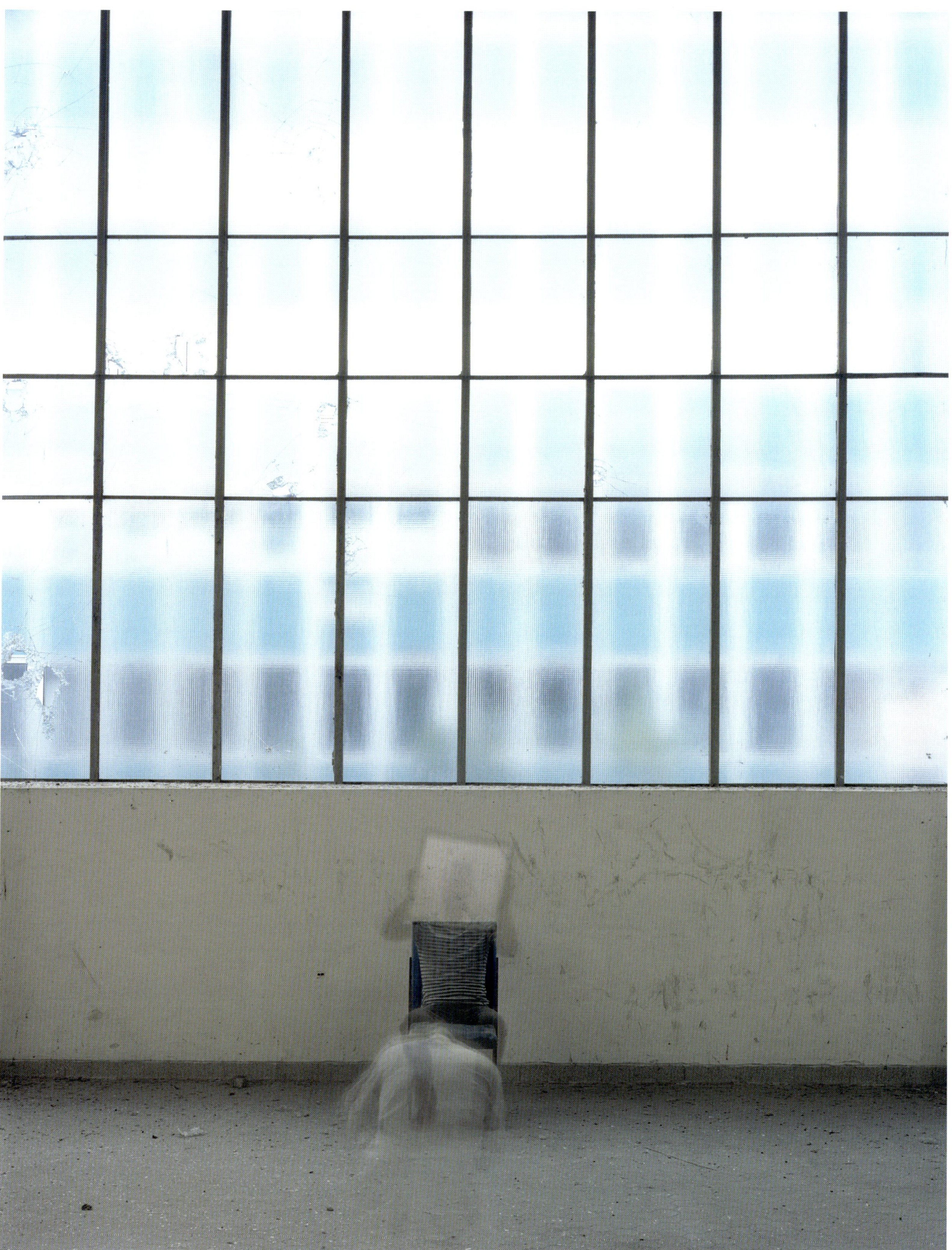

Falscher Himmel, 2012

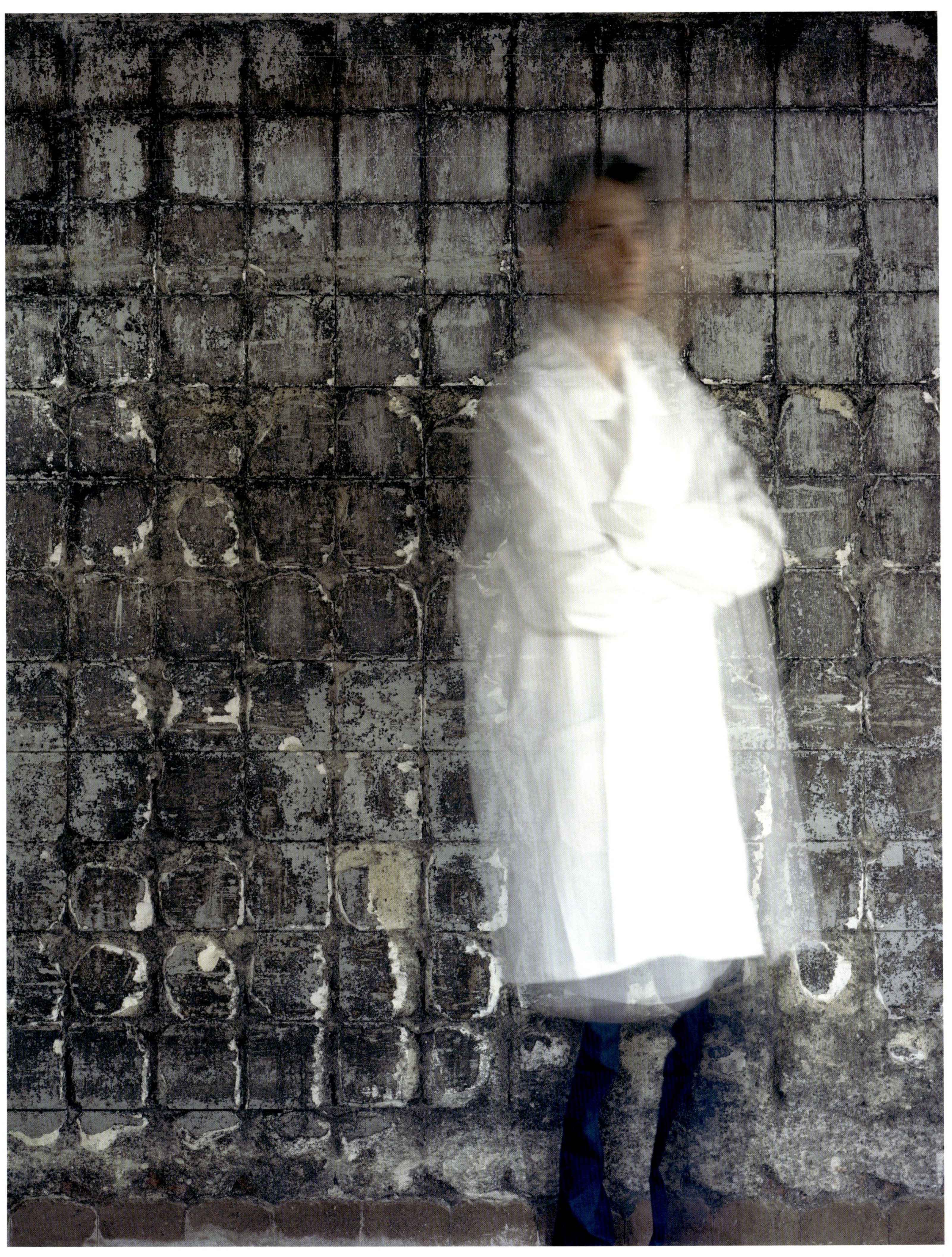

Self-Portrait, 2011 (detail)

Plates

Photographs by Andrej Pirrwitz

Suspension du temps

Andrej Pirrwitz pense ses images à partir de la fin. À partir des expériences liées à l'effondrement de systèmes politiques, d'industries vétustes et de sociétés en bout de course. À l'ère de la fin des rêves. Ses photographies matérialisent le temps immobilisé. Chacune d'entre elles est une image de l'obsolescence, immortalisée en pose longue. Les choses vont mal – pour nous, pour le monde, pour tout. En même temps, tout n'est pas perdu. Car ces images sont le résultat d'une conscience politique et d'un sens de la structure très pointus. Elles conquièrent un vide au goût de poussière de chaux. Elles sentent la faillite et l'abandon. Les lieux et les décors changent, mais la désolation demeure. Andrej Pirrwitz suit les coups d'une horloge sans cadran. Une force aveugle fait s'imbriquer passé et présent. Lénine n'est guère plus lu (p. 55), le prolétariat a déserté l'avant-scène et s'est réfugié dans la société de consommation. Chaises vides, bouteilles abandonnées et blouses de travail oubliées sont les éléments constitutifs de la solitude. C'est désormais acquis : dans l'Anthropocène, l'homme est occupé à s'éliminer lui-même, comme le décrit si bien Houellebecq. Au crépuscule de la misère, la pauvreté paralyse l'âme (p. 65). Mais la volonté d'art est omniprésente et produit des effets notables.

Andrej Pirrwitz ne franchit jamais la limite de l'atonalité ou de l'abstraction. Même en traversant le no man's land, son humeur reste bien tempérée. Les aperçus psychovisuels qu'il nous livre ne sont pas arbitraires, puisqu'ils vont au cœur même de la dynamique matérielle et structurelle. Par sa manière de mettre en images la réalité factuelle, il souligne que la vie est, littéralement, une question de point de vue, et que le positionnement de la caméra correspond à un choix existentiel.

Parfois, on aperçoit l'artiste lui-même sur la photo, ainsi dans son *Autoportrait* de 2011 (p. 13). Mais malgré sa présence dans l'image, il ne bascule jamais dans le réalisme documentaire. Debout devant un mur gris, isolé de son environnement et littéralement sans perspective, il fait partie intégrante de la composition picturale animée et arrangée, à la fois chercheur et poseur d'indices.

Andrej Pirrwitz visualise ses impressions du monde en reflétant ses propres expériences et en faisant correspondre à sa vision de la réalité ce qui se présente à lui. Volontiers labyrinthique. Toujours bien construite.

Contre la distanciation conservatrice de la pensée, sa sensibilité esthétique cherche à confronter les impondérables de l'espace comme une concaténation en profondeur. Ses observations et auto-observations donnent lieu à des mouvements exploratoires qui renvoient à des principes généraux.

Le spectateur ne peut jamais connaître avec certitude les endroits que l'artiste a parcourus. S'agit-il de l'architecture industrielle rationnelle du productivisme révolu ? Ou, venu du futur, l'artiste a-t-il deviné notre destin, qui est justement fonction de cette destruction capitaliste du monde ? Ses images sont-elles des prédictions ou des réminiscences ? Ou concernent-elles notre présent ? Sont-elles réalistes ou témoins d'un pessimisme culturel à toute épreuve ? Voire les deux ? Pour ma part, je n'y perçois aucun enthousiasme optimiste, mais plutôt une prise de conscience déprimante, à la fois précise dans ses détails et élégiaque.

Le sentiment de grande tranquillité qui se dégage de ces images se doit notamment à leur approche picturale, tout en retenue. Dans la mesure où l'artiste pratique aussi la peinture et la sculpture, il semble logique que dans son œuvre les dimensions atmosphériques se chevauchent et que la peinture et la photographie s'y répondent – tant pour ce qui est de leurs affinités thématiques que de leurs prémisses esthétiques. Les peintures d'Andrej Pirrwitz ne sont pas une réaction au développement de la photographie ou de la technologie numérique (comme les logiciels de résolution d'image) ; son travail tendrait plutôt vers la photographie comme dématérialisation de la peinture, ou vers la photographie comme peinture par d'autres moyens.

Ce qui distingue Andrej Pirrwitz, c'est sa spontanéité, une attention de tous les moments, qu'il vit au jour le jour sans verser dans la surexcitation. Ici et ailleurs. C'est cette attitude qui alimente la jauge atmosphérique de ses images, dans lesquelles le temps s'écoule lentement et qui nous confrontent à nos propres sentiments de perte, de peur et de tristesse.

Ces images sont diamétralement opposées à notre quotidien, où nous sommes entourés d'écrans luisants et assaillis de publicités criardes. C'est peut-être en cela que réside la vraie signification des moments narratifs distillés avec parcimonie par l'artiste.

Christoph Tannert
(Mars 2020)

Stillstellung der Zeit

Andrej Pirrwitz denkt seine Bilder vom Ende her. Aus den Erfahrungen des Zusammenbruchs politischer Systeme, abgewickelter Industrien und ruinierter Gesellschaften. In Zeiten ausgeträumter Träume. Diese Fotografien geben der stillgestellten Zeit eine Ausdrucksform. Jedes Bild ist eine Langzeitbelichtung des Vergänglichen. Es sieht verdammt schlecht aus mit uns und der Welt und mit allem. Aber irgendwie auch ganz gut. Weil diese Bilder das Ergebnis eines ausgeprägten politischen und eines Strukturbewusstseins sind. Sie erobern eine Leere, die nach Kalkstaub schmeckt. Es riecht nach Abbruch und Verlassenheit. Die Orte und Einstellungen wechseln. Die Trostlosigkeit bleibt. Pirrwitz orientiert sich an den Schlägen einer Uhr ohne Zifferblatt. Eine blinde Macht verklammert Vergangenheit und Gegenwart. Lenin wird kaum noch gelesen (S. 55), das Proletariat hat die Szenerie fluchtartig verlassen und ist in der Wohlstandsgesellschaft untergekommen. Leere Stühle, abgestellte Flaschen, vergessene Arbeitskittel sind konstituierende Elemente der Einsamkeit. Es ist vollbracht. Im Anthropozän ist der Mensch dabei, sich selber abzuschaffen, wie wir den Romanen von Michel Houellebecq entnehmen können. Im Halbdunkel der Mittellosigkeit friert die Armut Seele ein (S. 65). Aber der Wille zur Kunst ist da und zeigt ausgiebig Wirkung.

Dabei überschreitet Pirrwitz nie die Grenze zur Atonalität, zur Abstraktion. Selbst im Durchwandern des Niemandslandes bleibt er wohltemperiert. Was Pirrwitz an psychovisuellen Erkenntnisblitzen anbietet, ist nicht beliebig, sondern trifft das zentrale stoffliche und strukturelle Moment. Wie Pirrwitz das Faktische zur Anschauung bringt, unterstreicht, dass das Leben im wahrsten Sinne des Wortes eine Ansichtssache ist und die Position der Kamera eine existenzielle Haltung.

Vereinzelt sieht man den Künstler schemenhaft im Bild, etwa in seinem *Selbstporträt* von 2011 (S. 13). Er ist im Bildgefüge, ohne dass er plötzlich in einen griffigen Dokumentar-Realismus umspränge. Vor einer grauen Wand, isoliert von seiner Umgebung und buchstäblich ohne Perspektive, ist er Teil der animierten und arrangierten Bildkomposition, ein Spurensucher und Spurenleger zugleich.

Pirrwitz bringt seine Eindrücke von der Welt ins Bild, indem er seine Erfahrungen reflektiert und das Vorgefundene so aussehen lässt, wie es seinem Blick auf die Realitäten entspricht. Vorwiegend labyrinthisch. Immer gut gebaut.

Gegen den Sicherheitsabstand des Denkens sucht Pirrwitz' ästhetisches Sensorium die Konfrontation mit den Unwägbarkeiten des in die Tiefe geschachtelten Raumes. Beobachtungen und Selbstbeobachtungen münden in Suchbewegungen, die ins Allgemeine weisen.

Man kann sich nie ganz sicher sein, in welchen Locations sich der Künstler aufgehalten hat. Ist es die rationale Industriearchitektur der Maximalproduktion der Vergangenheit? Oder hat Pirrwitz, aus der Zukunft kommend, unseren Untergang gesehen, der aus genau dieser kapitalistischen Verheerung der Welt folgt? Handelt es sich um Vorblenden oder Rückblenden? Oder ist das unsere Gegenwart? Sind diese Bilder realistisch oder kulturpessimistisch? Oder beides? Ich sehe keinen optimistischen Enthusiasmus, dafür deprimierende Einsicht, präzise im Detail und elegisch in einem Atemzug.

Die große Ruhe dieser Bilder resultiert nicht zuletzt aus ihrer weichen, malerischen Anlage. Weil Andrej Pirrwitz auch Malerei und Skulptur zu seinen Arbeitsfeldern zählt, ist es naheliegend, dass es zur Überlagerung atmosphärischer Dimensionen kommt und Malerei und Fotografie aufeinander verweisen – in thematischer Verwandtschaft und bildästhetischen Prämissen. Andrej Pirrwitz' Malerei ist dabei nicht das Resultat der fotografischen Entwicklung bzw. der digitalen Möglichkeiten (etwa der Bildauflösung durch Computerprogramme), vielmehr offenbart sich in seinem Schaffen eine Tendenz hin zur Fotografie als Entmaterialisierung der Malerei bzw. einer Fotografie als Malerei mit anderen Mitteln.

Was Andrej Pirrwitz auszeichnet ist seine Spontaneität, sein Wachsein, das er ohne Überspannung lebt. Hier und anderswo. Damit füttert er das Stimmungsbarometer seiner Bilder, in denen die Zeit nur langsam vergeht und die uns mit unseren eigenen Verlustgefühlen, mit Furcht und Traurigkeit konfrontieren.

Diese Bilder sind das komplette Gegenteil zu unserem Dasein, in dem wir rund um die Uhr von flackernden Bildschirmen und bunten Werbeclips eingekreist sind. Vielleicht besteht gerade darin die Sinnhaftigkeit von Andrej Pirrwitz' wissend dosierten Erzählmomenten.

Christoph Tannert
(März 2020)

Putting Time on Hold

Andrej Pirrwitz thinks his images from the end. From the experiences of collapsing political systems, obsolete industries and ruined societies. At a time when there are no more dreams to dream. His photographs materialise time standing still. Each image is a long-exposure shot of obsolescence. Things are looking bad – for us, for the world, for everything. Well, maybe not all that bad. Because these images are the result of a sharp political and structural awareness. They conquer an emptiness that tastes of lime dust. They smell of termination and abandonment. The places and settings change but the desolation remains. Pirrwitz records the strikes of a dialless watch. A blind force merges past and present. Lenin is hardly read anymore (p. 55), the proletariat has fled the scene precipitously and found refuge in affluence. Empty chairs, abandoned bottles, forgotten work coats are the constituent elements of loneliness. Done and dusted. In the Anthropocene, man is about to abolish himself, as Houellebecq tells us. In the twilight of destitution, poverty freezes the soul (p. 65). But the will to art is ever-present and has far-reaching effects.

Pirrwitz never crosses the line towards atonality or abstraction. Even when wandering through the no man's land, he remains well-tempered. The psychovisual flashes of insight he offers us are by no means arbitrary, capturing instead the pivotal material and structural momentum. The manner in which Pirrwitz brings into view the facts underlines that life is literally a matter of perspective, and the position of the camera an existential attitude.

Occasionally, the artist himself can be glimpsed in the picture, for example in his *Self-Portrait* from 2011 (p. 13). But despite his presence, the image never lapses into gritty documentary realism. Standing in front of a grey wall, isolated from his surroundings and literally without perspective, he blends into the animated and arranged pictorial composition, simultaneously looking for clues and leaving clues for us to find.

Pirrwitz visualises his impressions of the world by reflecting on his own experiences and making the existing situation correspond with his personal view on reality. Predominantly labyrinthine. Always well-constructed.

Against the safe distancing of thought, Pirrwitz's aesthetic sensibility seeks to confront the imponderable nature of deep-layered space. Observations and self-observations result in exploratory movements that point us towards general principles.

Viewers can never know for sure which locations the artist has spent time documenting. Is it the rational industrial architecture of defunct productivism? Or has Pirrwitz, coming from the future, foreseen our doom, which ensues precisely from this capitalist devastation of the world? Are his images forecasts or flashbacks? Or is this our present? Are they realistic or culturally pessimistic? Or both? I do not see any optimistic enthusiasm here, rather depressing insights, at once precisely detailed and elegiac.

The great calmness of these images derives not least from their restrained, distinctly painterly approach. For an artist whose practice extends to painting and sculpture, it seems obvious that his work should manifest overlapping atmospheric dimensions and establish reciprocal relationships between painting and photography – as regards both their thematic affinities and aesthetic premises. Pirrwitz's paintings are not a reaction on the development of photography or digital technology (such as image resolution software); rather, his work evinces a tendency towards photography as a dematerialisation of painting, or towards photography as painting by other means.

What distinguishes Pirrwitz is his spontaneity, his alertness, which he lives out without unnecessary tension. Here and elsewhere. It feeds the atmospheric gauge in his images, in which time passes slowly and which confront us with our own feelings of loss, fear and sadness.

These images are the complete opposite of our existence, in which we are constantly surrounded by flickering screens and gaudy adverts. Maybe this is precisely where the meaningfulness of Pirrwitz's carefully dispensed narrative moments lies.

Christoph Tannert
(March 2020)

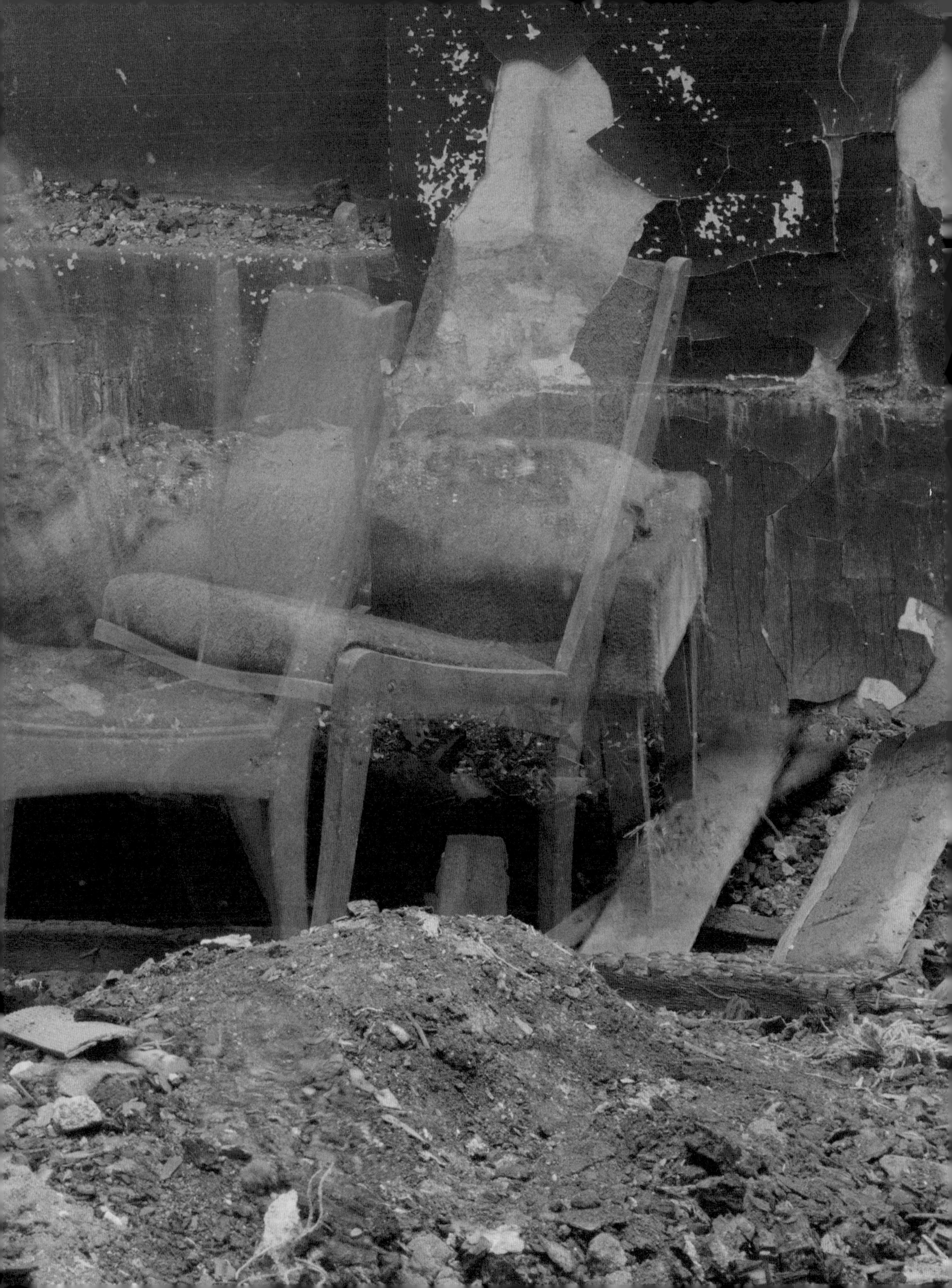

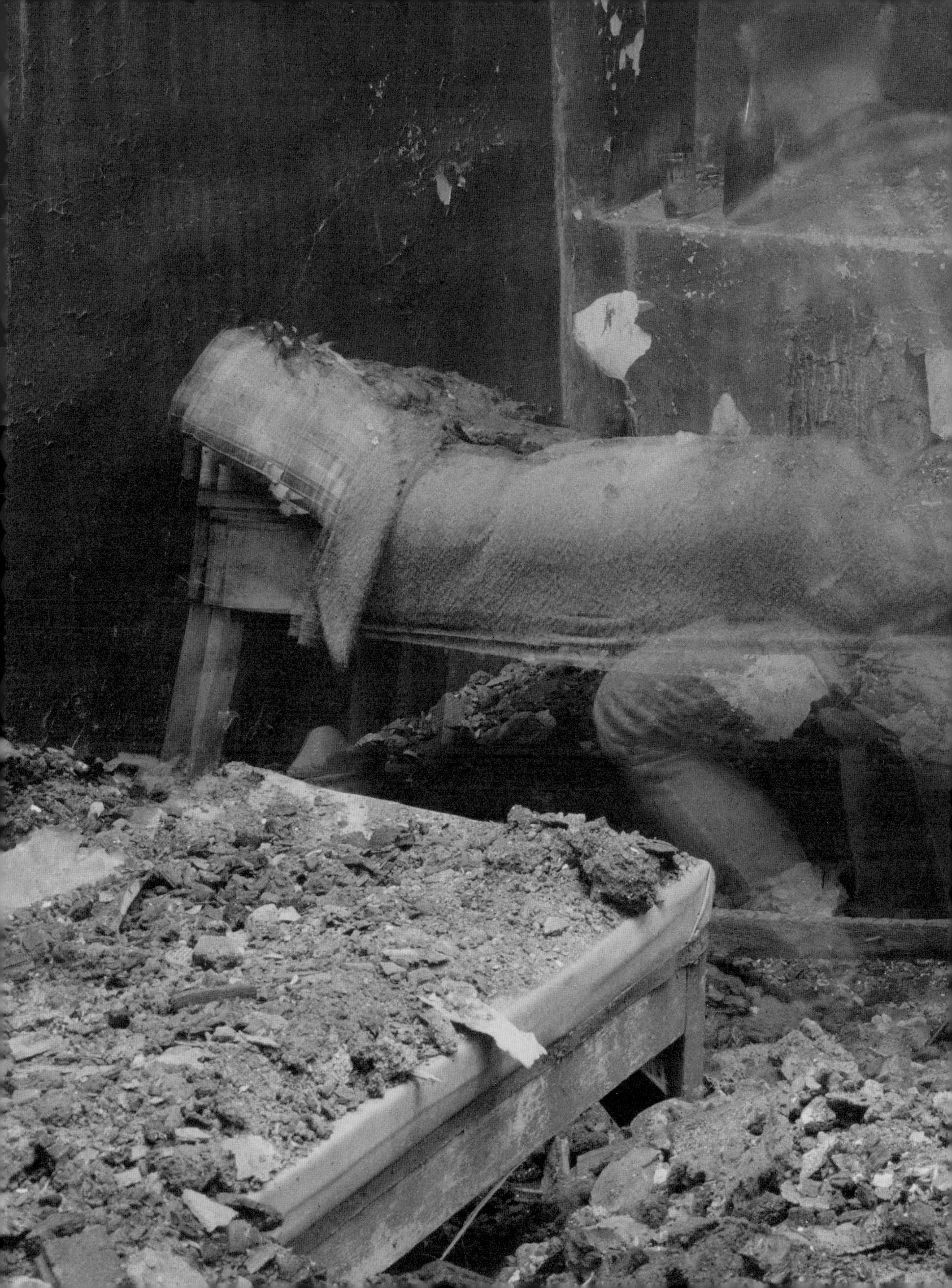

colours of soundlessness

Photographs by Andrej Pirrwitz

Text Christoph Tannert

andrej pirrwitz

colours of soundlessness

DISTANZ